LESSONS ON ROUSSEAU

LESSONS ON ROUSSEAU

Louis Althusser

Edited with an Introduction by Yves Vargas
Translated by G.M. Goshgarian

VERSO

This book is supported by the Institut français (Royaume-Uni)
as part of the Burgess Programme

Cet ouvrage publié dans le cadre du programme d'aide à la publication bénéficie
du soutien du Ministère des Affaires Étrangères et du Service Culturel de
l'Ambassade de France représenté aux États-Unis. This work received support from
the French Ministry of Foreign Affairs and the Cultural Services of the French
Embassy in the United States through their publishing assistance program.

First published in English by Verso Books 2019
First published as *Cours sur Rousseau*
© Éditions Le Temps des Cerises 2012
Translation © G.M. Goshgarian 2019

1 3 5 7 9 10 8 6 4 2

Verso
UK: 6 Meard Street, London W1F 0EG
US: 20 Jay Street, Suite 1010, Brooklyn, NY 11201
versobooks.com

Verso is the imprint of New Left Books

ISBN-13: 978-1-78478-557-4
ISBN-13: 978-1-78478-556-7 (HBK)
ISBN-13: 978-1-78478-559-8 (US EBK)
ISBN-13: 978-1-78478-558-1 (UK EBK)

British Library Cataloguing in Publication Data
A catalogue record for this book is available from the British Library

Library of Congress Cataloging-in-Publication Data
Library of Congress Control Number: 2019947020

Typeset in Garamond by Biblichor Ltd, Edinburgh
Printed and bound by CPI Group (UK) Ltd, Croydon CR0 4YY

Contents

Editor's Note on the Text   vii
Editor's Introduction   1

Lecture One   29
Lecture Two   63
Lecture Three   103

Index   141

EDITOR'S NOTE ON THE TEXT

THE TEXT THAT FOLLOWS is a faithful transcription of a course that Althusser gave in 1972 at the Paris École normale supérieure for students preparing to sit the *agrégation*. It is based on a tape recording made with Althusser's permission; he agreed to have a microphone placed on his lectern. Only a few words have been left out of the transcription: words that mark a hesitation ('well', 'uh', and so on), repetitions of the same word, and a few bits and pieces of sentences that were lost because a few seconds were needed to change the audio cassette. The reader may consult the original recording, which has been made available to the public by the Fondation Gabriel Péri.

Reading the courses edited by François Matheron and published by Le Seuil under the title *Althusser, Politique et histoire*, I was struck by the thought that this tape recording, which had been slumbering in my drawer for forty years, might serve as a source of ideas, suggestions for further research, and new knowledge not to be found in Althusser's 1956 and 1966 courses on Rousseau. That led to the deposit of the audio cassettes with the Fondation Gabriel Péri and publication of the present volume.

Editor's Introduction

TO TALK ABOUT A PHILOSOPHER who explains another philosopher is a paradoxical enterprise. Should one explain an explanation?

There should thus be no mistake about the objective of this introduction. Those who know Rousseau's texts well enough can read Althusser's course directly, and the same holds for those familiar with Althusser's thought.

The present introductory notes are meant for readers who are curious and attentive, but are not specialists, know the one philosopher and the other only by way of a few quotations or by hearsay, and might be discouraged by the rather abstract nature of the course or wearied by its repetitive features, forgetting that what is involved is a course intended for students taking notes, not a lecture intended for a public interested in acquiring information quickly. We have therefore extracted a few basic themes from the course, a few noteworthy original ideas, in order to provide a guide to a reading of it with the help of a few signposts, a few words, expressions and arguments that we have thrown into relief.

We have also attempted to reassess these remarks on Rousseau – which seemed remote, at the time, from Althusser's preoccupations with Marxism – by setting them in relation to his posthumous texts. Talking about Rousseau, Althusser was also talking to himself – as a reading, forty years later, of the pages on the 'materialism of the encounter' shows.

In these three lectures delivered in 1972, Althusser sets out to explicate a well-known text, Rousseau's *Discourse on the Origin and Foundations of Inequality among Men*,[1] a text elucidated many times before him. He proposes to analyse the 'less current' aspects of the text, for, he says, the history of philosophy 'has left these aspects aside' in 'drawing up its accounts' or 'settling its accounts'.

Rousseau's text

Rousseau's *Discourse on the Origin of Inequality*, as its title indicates, examines inequality, that is, political and social life, by setting out from the origin, that is, the period preceding the advent of society, in order to follow society's emergence and development with reference to this origin. This was a well-worn subject in the eighteenth century, in what was known as 'natural law philosophy' or, again, the 'philosophy of the Enlightenment'. Philosophers go back to the origin, before society, in the 'state of nature', and, on the basis of a discussion of this first state, they explain why society came into existence: since this state is not viable, since men kill each other in it (that is the 'state of war'), they have to leave it by agreeing to abolish the freedom to do what one likes and by making laws and choosing leaders to enforce them (that is the 'social contract'). Hobbes and Locke after him produced two different scenarios from this common stock, but this theoretical configuration (state of nature/state of war/social contract) forms the absolute horizon of Enlightenment thought: every philosopher, including Rousseau, thinks within this model. Many

---

1   Jean-Jacques Rousseau, *Discourse on the Origin of Inequality*, ed. Patrick Coleman, trans. Franklin Philip, Oxford: Oxford University Press, 2009.

different scholarly works (notably those by Robert Derathé[2] and Jean Starobinski[3]) have shown Rousseau's differences and borrowings from his predecessors; some scholars, surprised to see so many similarities between Rousseau and the others, had come to the conclusion that Rousseau is not at all original from a theoretical standpoint, and that his originality stems from the political uses he makes of theories in general circulation.[4] In his course, Althusser proposes to bring out the radical originality of Rousseau, who thought *in* the philosophy of the Enlightenment and *against* this philosophy, on the basis of a completely unprecedented philosophical dispositive. We shall see that Althusser does not study the usual 'Rousseauesque' questions (natural law, original goodness, the critique of different forms of despotism, and so on), but directs his attention to 'less concrete aspects' of Rousseau's thought.

Before approaching Althusser's lesson, let us take a look at the way Rousseau's *Discourse on the Origin of Inequality* presents itself. This text – often called the 'second Discourse' because it was preceded by the 'Discourse on the Sciences and the Arts' – has two parts. The first runs from the origin to the eve of society; the second treats the establishment of society beginning with the emergence of property. ('The true founder of civil society was the first man who . . . thought of saying, "This is mine."'[5]) In his course, Althusser basically discusses Part I, the pages in which Rousseau describes the origin before society ('the state of pure nature'). Here, Rousseau criticizes his predecessors for bungling this question: these philosophers ascribed to men in this supposedly natural state traits that are social, not natural (language, reason, property, the sense of honour, and so on), presupposing interhuman relations that were already social

---

2   Robert Derathé, *Jean-Jacques Rousseau et la science politique de son temps*, Paris: Vrin, 1970.

3   Jean Starobinski, *Rousseau, la transparence et l'obstacle*, Paris: Gallimard, 1971.

4   Bernard Groetuyssen, *Jean-Jacques Rousseau*, Paris: Gallimard, 1949 (published posthumously).

5   Rousseau, *Discourse on the Origin of Inequality*, p. 55.

(aggressiveness, mutual assistance). In short, they put society in nature: 'they talk of savage man and they paint civilized man'.[6] One must, then, avoid this mistake and 'dig down to the roots'[7] in order to describe a genuinely natural state, with men who are simply a sort of animal; they live scattered, without relations, without language or reason, and so on: men who roam all alone through the forest and sleep three-quarters of the time. Rousseau's text presents itself as a narrative, a sort of fictional vision that describes original man (Rousseau's famous 'good savage', who is so frequently evoked): a man living in solitude, peaceful, robust and naive, savouring a child-ish happiness; a sort of Eden that was to become the object of a celebrated gibe of Voltaire's, who felt the sudden urge 'to go on all fours' after reading the book. The *Discourse on the Origin of Inequality* quotes only a few authors and seems to want to avoid philosophical speculation.[8] Its descriptive style and simple diction have given rise to the idea of a visionary, utopian, romantic Rousseau, and it is classified more often as 'literature' than as 'philosophy' in school and college curricula.

The second part of the *Discourse* explains that this state of 'infancy' could well have gone on forever, but that natural catas-trophes, accidents, modified this first life, which became impossible (because of climatic change, the increasing scarcity of foodstuffs, and so on). Men were forced to gather in groups (families, villages, huts) and they forged connections with each other (to hunt big game, for example). This new life engendered new feelings: self-esteem (how others see me), imagination, reason. This second epoch, which Rousseau calls the 'youth of the world', is a first step beyond nature, a step, but just a step, and it would have been

---

6   Ibid., p. 24.
7   Ibid., p. 51.
8   Rousseau prides himself on sparing the non-specialist ('common') reader the philosophical questions that his observations raise. 'It is . . . enough for me to have set things out in a way that the common reader has no need to consider them at all.' Ibid., p. 54.

possible to remain there too for ever; things were not so bad that they had to be changed.[9] A 'fatal accident',[10] however, opened the third period: thanks to some chance occurrence (perhaps the eruption of a volcano), men discovered metallurgy, and the domestication of fire enabled them to clear land and invent agriculture; this led to a sort of system of economic exchange (a division of labour between metallurgists and farmers), a system that lasted as long as there was still land to be cleared.

The next section of the *Discourse* is about the origin of property, starting with the moment when all the available land had been cleared: some people (the 'rich') owned land, while others (the 'poor') owned nothing. At this point, a state of war began, for the poor sought to seize land for themselves, until the rich proposed a contract that put an end to the war and allowed them to keep their wealth: this is how inequality among men originated. There follows a description of political life, its corruption and slide towards tyranny. Althusser does not, however, analyse these pages in his course, confining himself to a few remarks about the return of the origin (state of nature) at the end of the process (the descent into tyranny).

As we have already said, Rousseau's text resembles a narrative, almost a novel, of human history;[11] an imaginary panorama inspired by travel narratives (the remote savages of the islands) and rounded off by Buffon's observations (Rousseau refers to Buffon in numerous notes): 'I see an animal less strong than some ... I see him eating his fill under an oak tree, quenching his thirst at the first stream ... What is true of animals in general is, according to the reports of explorers, true of most savage peoples as well.'[12]

---

9 'This period ... must have been the happiest and most enduring age ... This state was the best for man ... the human race was made to remain there forever ... this state was the true youth of the world.' Ibid., pp. 61–2.

10 Ibid., p. 62.

11 'O Man ... here, as I have read it, is your history ... in nature, which never lies.' Ibid., p. 25.

12 Ibid., pp. 26, 32.

Althusser's course

Althusser's course is not about the 'basic concepts' of Rousseauism, that is to say, natural law, human nature, food (fruit or meat), health, goodness, self-esteem, property, and so on.[13] Althusser takes up a problem in the margins of these concepts: that of the unfolding of history, that of the transition from one period to the next, from a present moment to its future. He treats the *Discourse on the Origin of Inequality* not as a narrative, but as a conceptual progression, a series of novel philosophical problems in search of solutions never before proposed. He presents the text as a series of links in a chain, commanded by what Rousseau posits at the outset: the true origin, 'the root', 'pure nature'. He goes on to show how each textual detail is a theoretical response to problems generated by this theory itself; what seemed to us to be mere stage decorations, *mises en scène*, or dramatis personae reveal themselves to be, as Althusser reads them, veritable philosophical concepts. There we have Althusser's 'signature', his distinctive trademark: he 'flushes out' concepts the way a hunter flushes out game and fashions new concepts in order to insert the theories that he establishes in them.

His three lectures break down as follows: the first is about the origin of society, the second examines the genesis of society, while the third returns to the state of origin and explains its coherence in detail.

What is striking about this approach to the text is that, far from presenting Rousseau's positions – his 'ideas', as one says – Althusser trains our attention on the problem commanding them, drawing out the distance between the problem and its solution as far as is

---

13   Victor Goldschmidt discusses all these concepts in *Anthropologie et politique: Les principes du système de Rousseau*, Paris: Vrin, 1974. Althusser says of Goldschmidt's book that 'there have been studies of the genealogies of these concepts (Goldschmidt's book is definitive), but there has not been enough study of the effects of this system as a whole'. Louis Althusser, 'The Underground Current of the Materialism of the Encounter', in *Philosophy of the Encounter: Later Writings, 1978–1987*, ed. François Matheron, trans. G.M. Goshgarian, London: Verso, 2006, p. 186.

possible and displaying all the threads which separate them, taut-
ened to the snapping point. Rousseau, to repeat, criticizes his
predecessors on the grounds that their 'origin' is already social and
that they have not attained the true origin. With this as his starting point, Althusser examines Rousseau's text to show that his
critique of other philosophers is posed in terms such that we can
no longer see how he can avoid the mistake for which he criticizes
others: for he criticizes them for making a mistake while simultaneously showing that this mistake was inevitable! Thus Rousseau
calls the use of reason into question, for reason is not natural but
social and is therefore incapable of grasping the state of nature. Yet
philosophy has no tool other than reason with which to think
anything at all, and if reason is invalidated, it is hard to see how it
could conceive of something that excludes it for essential reasons.
No one can draw a straight line with a skewed ruler, not even the
person who denounces the warp in the tool. Philosophy is caught,
Althusser says, 'in the *circle* of denaturation', from which it is
impossible to get out of with our faculties (reason, imagination,
and so on), which are themselves, as products of this denaturation,
caught in this 'circle'. How is one to free reason from this circle
that produces it, in order to think outside the circle, in order to
think true nature? Althusser, accordingly, presents Rousseau as
caught in the trap which he set for his predecessors, but which was
sprung on him: by invalidating *reason itself*, not just an *error in
reasoning*, he renders himself powerless. Rousseau 'leaves this circle
by way of the inside', Althusser explains, 'by going back into
[himself]' and listening to 'the voice of [his] heart'.[14] Althusser
wrests the Rousseauesque 'heart' from Romantic or intuitionist

---

14   In his 1966 course, Althusser affirms, according to an auditor's notes, that this
'solution is disarming: recourse to the heart'. Louis Althusser, *Politique et histoire: Cours
à l'École normale supérieure de 1955–1972*, ed. François Matheron, Paris: Seuil, 2006,
p. 304. In 1972, this 'solution' is not accompanied by a note of doubt. Let us point out
that the idea of the 'heart' is not explicitly present in the *Discourse on the Origin of
Inequality*, but is found in *Emile* and Rousseau's autobiographical texts.

interpretations of it in order to confer epistemological status on it: it is, within denatured nature itself, the voice of nature that will be able to guide reason. The heart is not one element among others in Rousseau's thought; it is the operative key to an impossible operation, the production of knowledge about true nature. There is more: by making reason dependent on the heart, by thus endowing it with secondary status, Rousseau 'marks himself off from', or 'takes his distance' from, the Enlightenment philosophy which posits reason as the fundamental, supreme principle. The 'heart' is thus not a thing – not even a deeply personal thing – but a theoretical operation, the consequence of which is a grasp of the true origin, the state of pure nature. 'Pure', in the expression 'state of pure nature', indicates – Althusser dwells on this – the difference from 'the state of nature' of which all the natural law philosophers speak. The 'heart' is a concept that operates on the object peculiar to it, and this object is 'pure' nature.[15] Althusser's first lecture thus situates Rousseau in his historical period and establishes the epistemological status of his concepts.

His second lecture is about the genesis of humanity, the genesis that leads to society as we know it. Here, too, Althusser sets about exacerbating problems. Once we have isolated the state of pure nature by leaving the 'circle of denaturation' (in which his preccessors were caught), it remains to see how, and by what means, it will be possible to turn back towards this denaturation (which has taken place; this is a fact, inasmuch as the state of pure nature no longer exists). Althusser, rather than quickly taking up the solution proffered by Rousseau (which we mentioned above: natural catastrophes, the discovery of metallurgy), subjects the state of pure nature to veritable philosophical torture in order to make it

---

15 Éliane Martin-Haag has worked this vein with remarkable success. She reconstructs Rousseau's 'system' on the basis of his biographical indications about his 'conscience', conceived as a sort of impetuous force of quasi-autonomous thought (Martin-Haag, *Rousseau et la conscience sociale des Lumières*, Paris: Honoré Champion, 2009).

confess, by all available means, that it is incapable, radically incapable, of producing society. It is as if Rousseau, after leaving the circle of denaturation by way of the heart, found himself caught in a second 'circle', that of the true origin, with no way of getting out of it. After seeking to formulate a true origin that expels every disguised trace of society, Rousseau walls himself up in a 'theoretical isolation' from which there is no exit: between this true origin and society he puts a 'distance', an 'abyss', a 'void created by this separation'.

That is the price to pay for this origin that is a 'radical absence [*néant*] of society'. A radical absence, not just an absence, for nothing indicates its absence, in the sense in which someone who is absent is waited for, has his name on a list: there is a place for him to take, which is empty while we wait for him, yet a place we can designate nonetheless. Althusser presents the state of pure nature as a present without a future, in a radical sense: the future is not a *necessity inscribed* in the present (what Althusser calls a 'deduction' – or 'analysis' – 'of essence'). We must, however, also understand that the future is just as plainly not a *possibility* of the present (a virtuality dependent on various elements contained in the present, which might, under certain circumstances, combine and fuse). Neither a necessity nor a possibility, the future is *the impossible of the present*. Historical time is thus divided, torn [*écarté, écartelé*] between a suspended present and 'its' future, from which it is absolutely separated (by an 'abyss').

On the basis of this hopelessly blocked situation, Althusser opposes the solutions of natural law philosophy (Hobbes, Locke) to Rousseau's. In Hobbes and Locke, society is deduced from the state of nature, since it is already present in it and its genesis is 'linear and continuous'; this is a 'deduction of essence'. For Rousseau, this genesis is the very opposite of a deduction; it can only come about thanks to chance occurrences and accidents that impinge on it from outside (catastrophes). It is a genesis made up of 'gaps', 'breaks', and 'hiatuses'. Ultimately, the state of nature finds itself 'dismembered' in three 'discontinuous moments'. The closed circle of the true origin (circle 1) is succeeded by other circles that are just as hermetically sealed: the youth of the world (circle 2) and nascent agriculture (circle 3).

This presentation of Rousseau's theory as riven by discontinuities [*en déchirure*] leads Althusser to define two points. The first is that Rousseau's philosophy proceeds by way not of right, but of 'history', the 'event': there is no appeal to right emanating from a fearful humanity (as there is in Hobbes, where men prefer to be subject to laws rather than risk death). Accidental, unpredictable fact changes everything and establishes a new order. The second point bears on the theory of this history: this Rousseauesque history is a combination of the accidental and the necessary. The accidents are contingent, but arrive 'at the right moment': there is 'coincidence between chance and the moment of chance',[16] and this establishes a rational, non-teleological history, because the necessity of the future has to wait for contingency. Althusser then comes back to these three 'circles' of the state of nature: pure nature (circle 1), youth of the world (circle 2), and metallurgy + agriculture (circle 3). If circles 2 and 3 are the result of a process, circle 1, in contrast, 'results from nothing' and 'is not the beginning', for 'the beginning begins [*ça commence*] after the origin'. Thus it comes from nothing and goes nowhere, as if suspended in the 'void'.

The rest of the second lecture examines this first state, paving the way for the following lecture, which will go into its contents in detail. Althusser puts this state under the general sign of negation: it is a 'radical absence of society', a 'radical absence of natural law', and

---

16   In *Emile*, there are many reflections on the question of the 'right moment'. In Book 5, for example, in connection with the encounter between Emile and Sophie, we read: 'Sophie was discovered long since; Emile may even have seen her already, but he will not recognise her till the right moment.' Jean-Jacques Rousseau, *Emile, or Education*, trans. Barbara Foxley, Indianapolis: The Online Library of Liberty, 2011, p. 331, translation modified.

it requires Rousseau to find a 'representation of negation'. Althusser explains that the 'realization' of this 'void' is provided by 'the forest', which is 'a void' 'without time', while human qualities in this state are themselves 'purely negative' (such as pity), or 'virtual', 'latent' (such as reason and perfectibility). This true origin is an 'origin of nothing' [*origine de rien*]; it is not the true double of the false origin, as in Plato, for whom error (the shadows at the back of the cave) is a deformed replica of reality (the light and the ideas outside).

The future is, at every moment in this history, not just absent from the present, but annihilated by a sort of antibody. The present abounds in anti-future; it is full of an antibody that voids the future, should it, perchance, present itself. The forest is this antibody, for it stuffs savage man full of everything he could feel a need for before he feels a need for it; it is a black hole that devours all causality in advance, with the result that there is no future in preparation or even in gestation. Thus 'perfectibility' does not strike root in the state of nature in order to bear fruit later, in society; 'perfectibility' is present, but for nothing, awash in an excessive fullness that drains it of all reality. We can learn only after the fact that it was present.[17] One measures the difference in tone between Rousseau's narrative, which is focused on savage man, his life, his acts, and his encounters, and Althusser's reading, which invests it with concepts and lines of force, a reading that is quite remote from the apparent 'novel'.

The remainder of the genesis, phases 2 and 3, is thus external to this 'origin of nothing', and the 'law of development' is specific to each phase, operating within each 'particular' circle. Each circle invents its own logic, fabricating its internal laws and problems for itself; they are not the same as those of the preceding or following

---

17   Althusser rejects the notion of human 'destiny', although Rousseau defends it. Althusser's reading annuls the Rousseauesque dispositive of the combination of causes (chance, mechanism, fatality). See Yves Vargas, 'Althusser-Rousseau: Aller-Retour', in *Rousseau et la critique contemporaine*, Études Jean-Jacques Rousseau, no. 13, Montmorency: Éditions du Musée Jean-Jacques Rousseau, 2002.

circles (for example, the origin of language is a problem that arises in the state of pure nature, but not in the youth of the world, while there is no place in the latter for the economic questions of labour, wealth, and so on, which will be at the centre of the next circle). Thus, according to Althusser, no general laws of history exist for Rousseau, but only regional laws that belong to each particular moment of history and yield to other laws in subsequent periods. We are at a very far remove from a Rousseau supposed to have anticipated Marxism with its universal economic laws (productive forces, relations of production, and so on).[18]

At the end of these three states of nature, the social contract makes its appearance. It is a 'leap in the void', suspended over an 'abyss', and a 'new beginning of the origin', a 'negation of the negation' ('denaturation of the denaturation'). For the social contract denatures man, but the man in question is the man of state 2 and state 3. These states, however, are themselves denaturations of state 1. Thus we do indeed have a denaturation of the denaturation.

The third lecture is more concrete: Althusser serves us notice that he intends to carry out a reading of the text itself, in order to analyse in detail that which makes it possible to think the state of pure nature. This state concerns, first of all, man's relation to nature, and, second, men's relations to each other. The former (man–nature) is an 'immediate' relation; 'man is at home' in nature because nature meets all his needs at all times and in all places. The latter (man–man) is 'nugatory', 'nil' [*néant*]; men live in dispersion, without contact, never seeing each other twice and

---

18 This explains Althusser's reservations about Engels' claim that 'in Rousseau . . . we find . . . a line of thought which corresponds exactly to the one developed in Marx's *Capital*'. Friedrich Engels, *Anti-Dühring (Herr Eugen Dühring's Revolution in Science)*, in *Marx and Engels Collected Works*, London: Lawrence and Wishart, 2010, vol. 25, p. 130.

forgetting each other as soon as they see each other. These relations make the state of pure nature possible, but are they themselves possible? That has to be demonstrated.

This demonstration implies a particular theoretical operation, for, says Althusser, to understand this Rousseauesque dispositive, we have to bring out certain concepts which are not 'thought' by Rousseau, although they are 'practised' by him; which are present in Rousseau, but in a state of 'theoretical divagation'. We must therefore go to work to pin them down and make them plainly visible, for Rousseau 'does not see them', he 'directs his gaze elsewhere', they 'escape his attention'. This holds for the concept of the 'accident', which is stated but not analysed as such; it holds, above all, for the 'concept of the forest', which is central: without it, the origin is unthinkable. Althusser replaces Rousseau's gaze, 'directed elsewhere', with another that makes it possible to see that the forest invented by Rousseau basically fulfils all the conditions required for the immediate fusion of man with nature (trees with low branches laden with fruit; shade; refuge), and also to see how the same forest separates men from each other (assistance is pointless, for the forest provides everything; war is impossible, for the forest offers protection and abundant nourishment). Setting out from this conceptual *mise en scène*, Althusser puts the elements of the theory back in place, bringing out its points of opposition to other theories (Hobbes, Pufendorf, Diderot, but also Aristotle). In this sense, his third lecture will seem more familiar to readers who know Rousseau; they will find a Rousseau they know in it, albeit displaced, highlighted, and redistributed.

Concepts at work

We must now go back over this description of Althusser's course in order to emphasize a certain aspects of it. First of all, the reader who reads through the *Discourse on the Origin of Inequality* before reading Althusser cannot help but notice one thing: certain *terms* that

Althusser uses are unmistakably Rousseau's, and here Althusser works on the standard text (for example, state of pure nature, pity, youth of the world, forest, needs, and so on); whereas other terms – terms that recur insistently throughout his exposition – are completely absent from the *Discourse on the Origin of Inequality* and even from other texts by Rousseau (for example, circle, nothingness, distance, void, negation of the negation, and so on). This remark about an obvious feature of Althusser's text leads us to oppose two levels of reflection: *explained* (Rousseau's text with its terms, the meaning of which has to be elucidated) and *explaining* (Althusser's discourse, with its invented terms that serve as tools with which to work on the first level). This might make it seem that we have to do here with the rather common situation of an 'explication of the text' that makes use of general categories to underscore the logic of an argument, along with its effects or its intentions. This way of looking at things is, however, incomplete, for in reality there are not two levels (Rousseau's terms/Althusser's terms), but three. Why three? Because the first level, that of 'Rousseau's terms', is itself situated on two levels, leading us to distinguish three levels.

1. There are, first, the terms (in reality, concepts) that operate in a way that the text takes responsibility for; they are at the centre of Rousseau's reflection and play an explicit theoretical role: nature, force, need, pity, perfectibility, and the like. All these concepts provide the core of the specialized studies of Rousseau.

2. There are, however, other terms (which are perhaps concepts, according to Althusser) that remain in the background to form a sort of accompaniment, prop, or punctual explanation: pure nature, the forest, accidents, and so on. Althusser says that Rousseau 'practises' these terms without 'seeing' them, because he 'directs his gaze elsewhere'. When we read his course, we notice that the leading role has been conferred on these backgrounded terms; they are the ones that traverse

Rousseau's text in order to indicate its coherence and unity. The example of the *forest* is noteworthy. In Rousseau's text, it seems to be nothing more than a stage-setting needed for the actors' performance; it is there simply to provide decor for the life of savage man. In Althusser's course, in contrast, the forest becomes the leading actor; it unfolds through the text's every detail, sustaining and producing it to the point that natural man, pure nature, and so on become nothing more than the shadows of the theoretical trees and fruit of the forest that grounds the entire edifice.[19]

3. It seems to us that this promotion of stage-setting-concepts or character-concepts results from the intervention of the last level (circle, void, nothingness, and so on) in Rousseau's text. It is as if this third level, rather than working on the text, slides beneath it in order to make its critical joints crack or to produce conceptual hernias: Althusser forges and uses these sub-concepts in order to display the fault-lines in the textual crust, to destroy its seeming continuity in order to set it on other foundations, on the ground of new concepts, on a new text of Rousseau's. In fact, it is the same text, but the roles have been inverted: the stage-setting has come to occupy the foreground.

The second level of reading is what we have called the conceptual 'promotion' of certain figures, the ones Rousseau 'practised' without seeing them because his gaze was 'directed elsewhere'. It seems to us that, at this level, Althusser has inaugurated a vast working programme for Rousseau studies, for he has shown the conceptual power of common objects (trees) or *mises en scène* (the

---

19   It is quite striking that none of the three pivotal concepts in Althusser's reading, the forest, the accident and the chance occurrence, is to be found in the excellent *Dictionnaire de Jean-Jacques Rousseau* (ed. R. Trousson and F.S. Eigeldinger, Paris: Honoré Champion, 2006), although it carefully combs through Rousseau's work to inventory more than 800 different terms.

non-fight under the fruit tree). Well before Gilles Deleuze put forward the notion of a 'conceptual persona',[20] Althusser had already worked it out, allowing us to 'see' that the epistolary exchanges in *The New Heloise* are a *mise en scène* of the concept of virtue, that the various *mises en scène* in *Emile* are so many references to certain laws of development of human history, that feminine sexuality is bound up with the theory of history, that Jean-Jacques Rousseau himself establishes his 'biographies' as the last experimental *mise en scène* of human nature and its denaturation. Althusser has assimilated the fictional and the picturesque in Rousseau to the stark order of systematic conceptuality. Many modern readers of Rousseau owe him a great deal.[21]

Let us begin with the third level, which corresponds to the body of Althusser's first lecture, the part following the introductory comparison of Machiavelli and Rousseau. What we are calling the 'third level' involves those concepts that are nowhere to be found in Rousseau's text and that Althusser constantly insinuates beneath it in order to reveal its fractures and moments of crisis. The first of these concepts is the *circle*, which is applied in various ways: Rousseau criticizes philosophers for conflating the state of nature and the state of society by inscribing social characteristics at the heart of nature, but adds that this mistake is grounded in reason,

---

20   Gilles Deleuze and Félix Guattari, *What is Philosophy?*, trans. Hugh Tomlinson and Graham Burchell, New York: Columbia University Press, 1994, p. 62.

21   Let us cite the most recent of them: Jean-Luc Guichet, who tracks the animal through the whole of Rousseau's work in *Rousseau, l'animal et l'homme*, Paris: Cerf, 2006; Luc Vincenti, *Jean-Jacques Rousseau, l'individu et la république*, Paris: Kimé, 2001; Blaise Bachofen, *La condition de la liberté: Rousseau critique des raisons politiques*, Paris: Payot, 2002; Bruno Bernardi, *La fabrique des concepts: Recherches sur l'invention conceptuelle chez Rousseau*, Paris: Honoré Champion, 2006; Florent Guénard, *Rousseau et le travail de la convenance*, Paris: Honoré-Champion, 2004; and Éliane Martin-Haag, who, setting out from the idea of 'conscience', reorients Rousseau towards a partial but radical materialism (*Rousseau ou la conscience sociale des Lumieres*, Paris: Honoré-Champion, 2009).

which is itself incapable of thinking anything other than society, since reason is not natural, but social. Althusser calls this argument 'the circle of denaturation' or 'alienation'. This figure of the circle goes well beyond the logical figure of the 'vicious circle', that is, of tautology or repetition of the same thing (A = A, social reason = society as represented by reason [*la société raisonnée*]).

Here, 'circle' indicates the absence of an outside or, to put it differently, the absence of a cause that would make it possible to leave the circle; it is an anti-Hegelian circle with no inner motor, a circle that can only go round and round for lack of an internal cause. If Althusser talks about a circle of denaturation containing a reason that is powerless to leave it, it is not in order to give a new name to the methodological tautology that Rousseau denounces, but to show the *impossibility* of leaving this circle – for Rousseau is trapped in his own critique and has no means of escaping it. The circle is neither a logical nor a topological figure, but a causal or, rather, anti-causal figure: Althusser uses the word 'circle' to designate a theoretical configuration that does not contain the causes of its own development. Every occurrence of the 'circle' later in his course is geared to this crisis of causality and leads to the same question: How to escape it, given that Rousseau has locked the exits without providing the keys? Thus, after the circle of denaturation which impedes the discovery of the state of nature, this state of nature, once it is mentioned by Rousseau, is described as a circle in its turn; the same holds for the state of the youth of the world and, finally, for that of metallurgy and agriculture. These three circles produce nothing but their recommencement, that is to say, nothing; each time, Althusser leaves his auditors waiting for a solution, a wait without an object, since this object, the cause they are waiting for, is not in the circle. Upon this wait, this 'suspense' that is a wait for no one knows what, Althusser constructs a scene of the *void*, of *absence*, of *deviation*, of *demarcation*, of *distance*, and even of the *abyss* (a term of Rousseau's that Althusser uses in a different sense).

Comparison of the courses of 1956 and 1966 with the present course (1972)

The figure of the circle that encloses a radical absence [*néant*] of causality seems to make its appearance rather late in Althusser's readings of Rousseau. In 1956, his course on Rousseau affirms, on the contrary, that he 'conceives of history as a process, as the effect or manifestation of an immanent necessity . . . It is not, however . . . a *continuous, linear development*, but a *nodal, dialectical process*.'[22] And again: 'Rousseau is perhaps the first philosopher to have systematically conceived of the development of history . . . as a development that is dialectically bound up with material conditions . . . (consider the forest, the end of the forest, the rich and the poor . . .).'[23]

We certainly do find a circle in the 1956 course, but it is the circle of tautology.[24] It appears clearly that Althusser, like most of Rousseau's Marxist readers, is looking for an internal ('immanent') historical causality in the *Discourse on the Origin of Inequality*, a history that progresses by sudden leaps and bounds ('dialectical nodal process') and is grounded on a material base ('the forest', and so on). The portrayal of a historical time on the verge of the abyss, empty of determinations, is not yet on the agenda.

Ten years later, in the 1966 course, the circle, the void, and nothingness all make their appearance. They do not, however, have the same systematic character; they are still associated with tautological forms and dialectical genesis. Certain formulas that the 1972 course puts at the centre of its reflection are to be found in the 1966 course, as are 'circles' separated by 'accidents'.[25] One

---

22   Althusser, *Politique et histoire*, p. 111.

23   Ibid., p. 113.

24   The 'circle of the social and legal theories which put at the origin of history, as its motor and principle, a reason that is in fact nothing but its result (consider also the circle of language)'. Ibid.

25   In 1966, we find 'transformation of contingency into necessity', 'a specific law

difference should be noted: in 1966, the internal relation between closure (circle) and the annihilation of history (the void) is not explicitly thought through; that is why, in 1966, the forest does not play the decisive role (causal antibody) that it will play six years later, in the course we are here concerned with.

Let us turn back to the 1972 course. It can be seen that the sub-concept of the *circle* and the sub-concepts of the *void, nothingness* [*néant*], and so on form a system: there is a causal void because the circle is a radical absence [*néant*] of internal causality ('radical absence of society'). The 'circle' makes it possible to eliminate recourse to the 'dialectic'. The term 'dialectic' is, moreover, absent from this course, except in a quotation from Engels, who finds 'in Rousseau . . . a whole series of the same dialectical turns of speech as Marx used'.[26]

Althusser, then, isolates the 'circles' that turn round and round for lack of an internal cause, and it is clear that this figure is constantly associated with the ideas of negation, the void, nothing, and so on. There is nothing in the circle that could get us out of it. Althusser's thought is fixed on a particular type of causality, the one we can neither predict nor expect nor guess, for it is an 'accident' – a term of Rousseau's that he elevates to the rank of a master concept. It is likewise in order to produce the void – to show clearly that, in the circle, there exists no cause, however slight, that might make it possible to leave it – that Althusser is led to establish the *forest* as a concept: for the forest is perceived as the a priori suppression of anything that might open up the circle, so that there is not only nothing in the circle, but also a painstaking construction of this nothing. The forest is a 'concept' because it is the incessant, painstaking fabrication of this nothing; it puts, everywhere, a void between every

<hr/>

governing each of its phases' ('Rousseau et ses prédecesseurs', in *Politique et histoire*, pp. 308–9). A graphic representation may be found in ibid., p. 300.
26 Engels, *Anti-Dühring*, p. 130.

thing and what follows that thing; it blocks every embryonic form of causality in advance.

By creating the void around the circles and in them, Althusser makes room for a theory of history at antipodes from the 'dialectical' tradition that depicts historical time as an unfolding of the contents, the 'internal contradictions', that produce their sublation. There is no contradiction in the Althusserian circles; history becomes inseparable from the idea of the event, that is, an unpredictable accident that occurs at the right moment. It would be a mistake to suppose that the passage about the 'negation of the negation' ('denaturation of the denaturation') suggests a kind of dialectic, *à la* Engels. For, in this passage, Althusser defines the social contract as a negation of the negation on the grounds that man's entry into political society necessarily denatures him (Rousseau repeats this in several texts). As we noted, however, this denaturation pertains to a previous state (youth of the world, agriculture) that is itself a denaturation with respect to true (pure) nature. It is, for this reason, a denaturation of denaturation. In this formula, however, the negation of the negation, far from being the motor that goes from the present to the future (from pure nature to society), is, rather, a return of the present towards the past for the purpose of recovering that past *après coup*. Althusser calls this a 'reprise' [*reprise*]. Society takes back [*reprend*] from nature what nature never gave it. Thus there is a return of (towards) pure nature, but not at all in accordance with a dialectical spiral advancing all by itself. Quite the contrary: Althusser takes note of a return or reprise of something that was without effect, without dynamics, without progress – it is simply noted. One sees what Rousseau owes to Althusser: a reading that transforms his figures (images, characters, stage-settings, situations, and the like) into veritable concepts and a theory of history that is materialist but not dialectical.

What Althusser owes to Rousseau

In considering Althusser's three courses on Rousseau (1956, 1966, 1972), we have seen that he gradually takes his distance from what might be called the traditional Marxist reading of Rousseau. Obviously there exist Marxist readings that are highly divergent in their interpretations, but they generally revolve around the same preoccupations. Rousseau is a 'petty bourgeois' thinker (a reading directly inspired by Marx), a dialectician (Engels), a socialist who anticipated Marx, and so on. Generally speaking, Marxists look for a dialectical 'method' in Rousseau, an economic determinism, a body of political thought centred on the state or on equality, an anthropology that opposes man and the citizen: they look for Marx in Rousseau either to find him there or to remark his absence.[27] While Althusser's 1956 text fits into this theoretical landscape rather well, his 1966 text detaches itself from it, and his 1972 text has nothing more to do with it.

------

27   Here are a few quotations that provide something of an idea of the theoretical tone: 'It is Rousseau's merit to have sketched a method that is already dialectical, the history of society' (Jean-Jacques Lecercle, Introduction to *Discours sur l'origine de l'inégalité*, Paris: Éditions sociales, 1965, p. 42). 'Marxism–Leninism takes note of Rousseau's egalitarian claim for recognition of every merit and personal condition' (Giovanni Della Volpe, *Rousseau and Marx*, trans. John Fraser, London: Lawrence and Wishart, 1978, p. 91). 'Rousseau's doctrine, in spite of its entirely erroneous conceptions, played an important revolutionary role during the French Revolution' (Nikolai Bukharin, *Historical Materialism: A System of Sociology*, translation of the third Russian edition, New York: Russell and Russell, 1965, p. 96). 'Marxist . . . analysis has nothing to do with Rousseau's, except that it attempts to solve the problem which Rousseau posed, the problem . . . of the *social bond*' (Henri Lefebvre, *De l'État*, vol. 3, Paris: UGE 10/18, 1977, p. 53). 'Rousseau, Marx, and Lenin have shown that freedom can only be achieved in and through society, and that it is by transforming society that we attain freedom' (Guy Besse, 'De Rousseau au communisme', *Europe*, nos 391–2, December 1961, 'Jean-Jacques à 250 ans', p. 177). 'It is Rousseau who expressed this in his second Discourse, by showing that social conditions (that is, people's interrelations) depend on economic conditions (that is, people's relationship to nature') (Louis Althusser, 'Les problèmes philosophiques de l'histoire' [1955], in *Politique et histoire*, p. 175).

In 1972, there is no longer any question of the dialectic and, as we have emphasized, the 'negation of the negation' is the very opposite of what Engels designates by that term, since, rather than being a future-orientated process, it is merely the retrospectively observed 'reprise' of an inactive past. The economic problems have disappeared, and the whole course concentrates on hermetic circles emptied of causality, the happen-stance of unpredictable accidents, and the retrospective theory of history, which breaks with the monism of laws that constituted the foundation of the historical and dialectical materialism in general circulation; it is not a question of either class struggle or productive forces (elements that are, however, easy to exhibit in Rousseau's text when one sets out from simple identifications: the rich/the poor, forced labour, and so on). Thus Rousseau appears to be at a rather far remove from Marxism, and Professor Althusser seems oddly distant from the communist philosopher who gained his international reputation on the strength of an analysis of the writings of Marx, Lenin, and Mao.

A reading of Althusser's posthumous texts and his correspondence shows that this is not the reality of the matter, and that, in 1972, Althusser was thinking about the question of materialist philosophy in accordance with a twofold idea.

On the one hand, he was fabricating 'his own Marx'[28] by repeating the classical terms of Marxism in order to confer new content on them. He poured new wine into old bottles, keeping the words but investing them with a meaning that allowed him to develop a

---

28   'I had invented my own . . . Marx . . . far removed from the real Marx . . . I suppressed everything which seemed incompatible with his materialist principles . . . esp. the apologetic categories of the "dialectic", and even the dialectic itself.' Louis Althusser, *The Future Lasts Forever* and *The Facts*, ed. Olivier Corpet and Yann Moulier Boutang, trans. Richard Veasey, New York: The New Press, 1993, p. 221.   •

new theory of historical causality.[29] He rejected materialism's ontological preoccupations (matter precedes thought, and so on) in order to found materialism on a theory of knowledge and, later, on a theory of the primacy of practice. All this is rather well known.

On the other hand, he already had this 'Rousseauesque' depiction of nothingness, the unpredictable encounter, circumstance, retroactive [après-coup] causality, and the like in mind, as is attested by his correspondence when, in 1971, a year before delivering this course, he wrote to his friend Franca: 'Encounter: this word is very important for me, and has a profound resonance: I'm holding it in reserve for philosophical interventions about the dialectic that I will make some day.'[30] We can also discern a few formulations of this line of thought in his lecture on Lenin: 'The intervention of each philosophy, which displaces or modifies existing philosophical categories . . . is precisely the philosophical nothing . . . since a dividing-line is actually nothing; it is not even a line, but *the emptiness of a distance taken*.'[31] Above all, his posthumous autobiography sheds light on this development. He evokes the 'materialism of the encounter' in these terms in it: 'I typed (between November 1982 and February 1983) a two-hundred-page philosophical manuscript which I have kept . . . Actually, I expressed for the first time in writing a certain number of ideas I had carefully stored away in my mind for over twenty years, ideas I told no one else about as they seemed so important to me (!).'[32] These important ideas are those of the materialism of the encounter, the 'underground current' whose resurgence he wished to reveal. He attributes it to

29   See Yves Vargas, 'L'horreur dialectique (description d'un itinéraire)', in Jean-Claude Bourdin, ed., *Althusser: Une lecture de Marx*, Paris: Presses universitaires de France, pp. 147–92.

30   Louis Althusser, *Lettres à Franca (1961–1973)*, Paris: Stock/Imec, 1998, p. 784.

31   Louis Althusser, 'Lenin and Philosophy', trans. Ben Brewster, in *Philosophy and the Spontaneous Philosophy of the Scientists and Other Essays*, ed. Gregory Elliott, London: Verso, 1990, p. 197.

32   Althusser, *The Future Lasts Forever*, p. 268.

Epicurus and Democritus, but it is Rousseau who reactivates it,[33] and Althusser partially reincorporates his 1972 course into this hastily written text.

There can be no question of presenting this new philosophy here.[34] We shall restrict ourselves to displaying its themes, which echo the course on Rousseau that concerns us here. A few quotations will indicate the tone of it, while bringing out the radical difference between this materialism and the (mechanistic or dialectical) materialist tradition which, as is well known, is a thought of necessity, determinism, and the laws of Being.

My intention, here, is to insist on the existence of a materialist tradition that has not been recognized by the history of philosophy. That of Democritus, Epicurus, Machiavelli, Hobbes, Rousseau (the Rousseau of the second *Discourse*), Marx and Heidegger, together with the categories that they defended: the void, the limit, the margin, the absence of a centre, the displacement of the centre to the margin (and vice versa), and of freedom. A materialism of the encounter, of contingency – in sum, of the *aleatory*.[35]

This philosophy is, in sum, a philosophy of the *void* . . . a philosophy which *creates the philosophical void* in order to endow itself with existence . . . philosophy's 'object' *par excellence* is nothing, nothingness, or the void.[36]

---

33   'It is to the author of [Rousseau's second Discourse or the "Discourse on the Origin of Languages"] that we owe another revival of the "materialism of the encounter".' Althusser, 'The Underground Current', pp. 183–4.

34   See especially Jean-Claude Bourdin, 'Matérialisme aléatoire et pensée de la conjoncture: Au-delà de Marx', in Bourdin, *Althusser*, pp. 193–228. See also Annie Ibrahim, ed., *Autour d'Althusser: Le matérialisme aléatoire*, Paris: Le Temps des cerises, 2012.

35   Louis Althusser, 'Philosophy and Marxism: Interviews with Fernanda Navarro, 1984–1987', in *Philosophy of the Encounter*, p. 261.

36   Althusser, 'The Underground Current', pp. 174–5.

This void is clearly the one that Althusser reveals in his interpretation of the theory of history in Rousseau; it is the radical absence of the future at the heart of the present, the absence of any general law that might make it possible to trace the contours of a possibility. The real is thus nothing other than the consequence of 'accomplished facts', of 'encounters', of 'contingency'; necessity (which is so important in the schema of traditional materialism) is simply thought's return to the absolutely unpredictable accomplished fact, which it takes up again in order to establish its necessity. The historical real invents its laws, while thought boards 'a moving train' and adapts to its rhythms in order to understand those laws after the fact.[37]

The posthumous text ("The Underground Current') declares its debt to Rousseau at length:[38] 'The most profound thing in Rousseau is doubtless . . . this vision of any possible theory of history, which thinks the contingency of necessity as an effect of the necessity of contingency, an unsettling pair of concepts . . . explicitly postulated in Rousseau.'[39]

In these pages, written in haste, we find Althusser's 1972 Rousseau again, with, however, certain differences. In the course on Rousseau, it is the notion of the 'circle' which assigns the 'void' and 'nothingness' their theoretical status, for this void is the void of causality, bound up with an immobile, self-enclosed stage with no outside; the void is a confinement. In the text on the materialism of the encounter, the circle breaks open, freeing the void and nothingness, which pour out into the whole of the thinkable real,

37 'He always catches a moving train, the way they do in American Westerns. Without knowing where he comes from (origin) or where he's going (end). And he gets off somewhere along the way.' Althusser, 'Portrait of the Materialist Philosopher', *Philosophy of the Encounter*, p. 290.

38 In contrast to the text published in Mexico in 1987 ('Philosophy and Marxism') which, oddly, seems to ignore this debt.

39 Althusser, 'The Underground Current', p. 187. On the 'necessity/contingency' relation, see Kenta Ohji, 'Nécessité/contingence: Rousseau et les Lumières selon Althusser', *Revue Lumières*, no. 15/1, 2010.

constituting not a particular figuration (state of nature, and so on),
but philosophy as such. Rousseau's theory is now shorn of its
'circles', which had provided it with its frame. The example of the
forest is revelatory. In the 1972 course, the forest shields the circle
of pure nature and puts a brake on all human evolution; in the text
on the materialism of the encounter, however, it becomes a general
paradigm of the void, an Epicurean void with no encounters
between the atoms and no encounters between people. It had been
an excessive fullness of food and an excessive fullness of shelter
that ruled out the social, a natural excessive fullness that was a
'radical absence of society', inconceivable without the hypothesis
of a pure, self-enclosed nature. In the following quotation from
'The Underground Current', in contrast, we see the 'radical absence
[*néant*] of society' escape from the circle of pure nature, to be
transformed into the 'essence of all society'. In the course, however,
this essence had not proceeded from 'nothingness' [*néant*], since
this nothingness was not an 'origin of nothing': but, rather, from
an utterly heterogeneous accident which, far from proceeding
from this nothingness, put an end to it. Here is the posthumous
passage on this question: 'The forest is the equivalent of the Epicurean
void in which the parallel rain of the atoms falls . . . In this way,
Rousseau seeks to represent . . . a *radical absence of society* . . . the
radical absence of society constitutes the essence of all society.'[40]

    In the materialism of the encounter, there is no longer any room
for the circle, and Althusser seems to abandon this figure, which
constitutes the topological basis for his course.[41] We find it again,
by chance, in his autobiographical narrative, when he discusses

---

    40   Althusser, 'The Underground Current', pp. 184–5.

    41   It should, however, be noted that this abandonment of the circle modifies the
vision of history: it is no longer a matter of accidents external to society which come
from without to perturb it, but of 'encounters', that is, of independent causal series
whose conjunction is not given in advance (Cournot's theory, to which Althusser
alludes, ibid., p. 193). Historical causality is thus clearly inside the system this time; we
move from the impossible future of the circle to a possible but unpredictable future.

his experience of captivity in Germany: just as Rousseau leaves the circle of denaturation by way of the inside (the heart), the prisoner-of-war had thought up a plan to escape by hiding in the very heart of the camp.[42]

More seriously, in 'Is it Simple to Be a Marxist in Philosophy?', Althusser criticizes the notion of the circle, which he considers to be too Hegelian to suit materialism: 'a circle is closed, and the corresponding notion of totality presupposes that one can grasp all the phenomena, exhaustively, and then reassemble them within the simple unity of its centre'.[43]

In contrast, the theme of the multiple laws of history specific to each period is forcefully taken up again, with its theoretical complement (already present in the course) of retroaction [*l'après-coup*]: 'No determination . . . can be assigned [otherwise] than by *working backwards* from the result to its becoming, in its retroaction . . . we must think necessity as the becoming-necessary of the encounter of contingencies . . . every historical period has its laws.'[44]

Thus each of the sub-concepts that allow Althusser to reveal the neglected fabric (Rousseau directs his gaze elsewhere) of Rousseau's theory derive from these ideas that he had in mind but confided to no one. They allow him to construct 'his Rousseau',[45]

---

42   'My earlier problem of wanting to escape: how to get out of the camp while remaining there' (Althusser, *The Future Lasts Forever*, p. 206). It was a matter of hiding somewhere in the camp for three or four days while waiting for the end of the manhunt, in order to flee in the real sense.

43   Louis Althusser, 'Is it Simple to Be a Marxist in Philosophy?', trans. Grahame Lock, in *Philosophy and the Spontaneous Philosophy of the Scientists and Other Essays*, p. 220.

44   Althusser, 'The Underground Current', pp. 193–4, 195.

45   In connection with this 'underground current of materialism', Althusser carefully stipulates, in citing Rousseau, that he means 'the Rousseau of the second *Discourse*'. This is understandable, for Rousseau attempts, in his way, to think the contingency that arrives 'at the right moment'; he does so, however, by mixing up finalism with mechanism in a sort of makeshift causality. It is in *Emile* that Rousseau develops this confused theory of history.

just as he constructed a Marx all his own. Rousseau is an experimental field from which he makes nothingness, the encounter, retroaction, and so on surge up: so many non-Rousseauesque categories that nevertheless fit Rousseau to perfection: 'It is to the author of the second *Discourse* . . . that we owe another reprise of the "materialism of the encounter".[46]

The word is, unmistakably, reprise, which plainly means that it is a question of a retroactive encounter, not a continuity. Rousseau took up the materialism of the encounter in the sense in which the materialism of the encounter took up Rousseau, thereby opening up a field of reading that is still largely unexplored.

Yves Vargas, May 2012

---

46   Althusser, 'The Underground Current', pp. 183–4, translation modified.

LECTURE ONE

25 February 1972

L AST TIME, I ANNOUNCED THAT I was planning to give you a lecture, or a few lectures, on the conception of law [*droit*] and politics in Spinoza. In reading up a little on the question, however, I discovered that an excellent work on it has been out for several months now: Matheron's doctoral thesis, *Individu et communauté chez Spinoza*.[1] If I were to take on this question, I wouldn't do much more than reproduce, basically, what Matheron has written. That's why I thought it would be more helpful to talk to you about another subject, another author, and to submit a few, less common, reflections on Rousseau to you.

Changing programmes is, obviously, a high-handed procedure. Please accept my apologies, but I didn't have much choice: I'm not as competent as all that. I can really only talk about subjects I know at least a little and, for many authors, that is not the case. It is the case, somewhat, for Rousseau. So, after talking to you about Machiavelli, I shall try to talk to you a little about Rousseau.

---

1 Alexandre Matheron, *Individu et communauté chez Spinoza*, Paris: Minuit, 1969.

To talk about Rousseau after talking about Machiavelli is not just to change periods, since it means crossing two centuries of history and, in particular, two centuries of natural law philosophy, but it is also to change worlds. It is a matter not just of changing historical worlds, but of changing theoretical worlds too – of changing, quite precisely, the object of reflection and, still more, the form of reflection, the form of thought, the modality of thought. From that standpoint, in order to bring out these differences, however paradoxical the idea may seem, it is perhaps not without interest to compare Machiavelli's world in thought to the natural law philosophers' and Rousseau's.

I think we can regard the following condition as determinant and as a distinguishing criterion: what is at issue, what is at stake and in question in Machiavelli as well as the natural law theorists is absolute monarchy as a form of realization of the nascent and the developed bourgeois nation – and thus as an objective referent common to their different histories. In Machiavelli, however, that same historical referent plays a role altogether incommensurable with its role in the natural law theorists. That is what makes their theoretical worlds different; for the absolute monarchy does not occupy the same place in them. The absolute monarchy does not have the same significance as object in them, and that is why their worlds are not the same. We could say that, like Pascal's sea, which changes because of a rock,[2] the political, theoretical, and philosophical worlds of Machiavelli and the natural law philosophers change because of a mode, because of the modality of existence of the object that absolute monarchy, absolute political power, comprises in their thought.

To mark this difference, we can say the following: Machiavelli's world is one in which the absolute monarchy, the national state,

---

2   'The least movement affects all of nature: the whole sea changes because of a rock.' Blaise Pascal, *Pensées*, trans. and ed. Roger Ariew, Indianapolis: Hackett, 2004, p. 281.

exists not as a real, existent, instituted object, but as a political
objective to be realized. For Machiavelli, in other words, national
unity is not an accomplished fact, but *a fact to be accomplished*. We
have already shown that Machiavelli's thought in its entirety is
geared to this task, the task of constituting a new state under a new
prince in order to bring about national unity. We have also shown
that, for defined political reasons, Machiavelli's thought had to set
itself the altogether unprecedented, radical theoretical task of
thinking the conditions of possibility of the existence of that
which does not yet exist: that is to say, the task of *thinking radical
beginning*. For, since the initial political basis for national unity
was nowhere in existence, it was necessary that it begin; it was
necessary to create it. Thus it was necessary to think its absolute
beginning; it was necessary to define the conditions of possibility
of this absolute beginning. The consequence is that Machiavelli's
object, absolute monarchy, exists in the mode of the political
objective, of a political objective. Machiavelli has to think this
object under exceptional theoretical conditions that can be
summed up as follows. On the one hand, he has to think the fact
to be accomplished, he has to think in the fact to be accomplished,
in the element of the fact to be accomplished, in the question of
the fact to be accomplished. On the other hand – this comes
down to the same thing – Machiavelli has to think the beginning
as such, and he has to think in the beginning, in the element of the
beginning, in the element of the question of the beginning, and so
on. There you have the two decisive terms: the fact to be accomplished and the beginning.

Should we say that these two words are two concepts? I shall
leave the question in abeyance and say that, even supposing that
they are two concepts, these two words are in any case complementary; they define what might be called both the object and the form
of Machiavelli's thought, his specific form of thought. We may add
that, in their conjunction, the fact to be accomplished and the
beginning are played, in the musical sense of the word, if you like, as

if they were the score of a silent philosophy, a philosophy that has not succeeded in expressing itself in philosophical form, the score of a philosophical beginning that has never taken place because no one has ever noted its existence. Thus it is no wonder that Machiavelli should have remained a stranger to all philosophy, to classical philosophy; it is no wonder that dominant and even dominated classical philosophy should have taken Machiavelli to be foreign to philosophy and left him out of account. For that matter, if we consider classical philosophy for a moment, has it ever, for its part, thought in the pair formed by the fact to be accomplished and the beginning? Has that philosophy ever attempted to think the fact to be accomplished and the beginning?

The situation of natural law philosophy is obviously completely different from the situation of Machiavelli's not-yet-philosophy. Natural law philosophy is dominated by a completely different question. The reason is simple: in the world of these theorists, absolute monarchy or national unity was an accomplished fact – if not a wholly accomplished fact, then, at least, an irreversible fact on its way to being accomplished on perfectly well-known, perfectly well-defined political bases, the history of which shows that they were in the process of expanding sufficiently to accomplish their mission. And, from this simple fact, which still concerns the same referent, but in another mode, there results a first radical difference from Machiavelli.

These natural law theorists think in the accomplished fact; they think the accomplished fact. That, of course, does not prevent them from taking, in their theories, political positions on this accomplished fact of the absolute monarchy: for example, by declaring or demonstrating, like Hobbes, that they are absolutists (in other words, partisans of the monarchy, of the dictatorship of the absolute monarchy in the development of the first forms of bourgeois capitalism); or, like Locke, in a later phase, by declaring that they are liberals; or, like Rousseau, by declaring that they are democrats. At any event, the pros and cons with respect to the accomplished fact, as well as the 'cons' directed against certain forms of the 'pro' – all these positions observable in the history of natural law are adopted in the element of the accomplished fact. They have nothing to do with Machiavelli's problematic of the fact to be accomplished.

All this has, consequently, nothing to do with Machiavelli's question of questions, the question of the beginning. When natural law theory enters, Machiavelli exits; or, rather, we realize that he never made his entrance onto this scene. He was, always and for all time, somewhere else. Thus natural law philosophy thinks the accomplished fact and in the accomplished fact: its object and its form of thought will be determined, as I shall to try to show, in a way quite different from the way Machiavelli's object is.

Natural philosophy's object will be political power not as a task to be accomplished, not as a contingent relationship of being to nothingness, nor as event or beginning; rather, its object will be political power as existing, as existent [*étant*], and this object will be thought in the categories of the existent and the essence of the existent. Natural law philosophy accordingly discusses society, civil law and public law not in terms of chance occurrence and encounter, of event and advent, but in terms of existence and essence. It relates these essences (of natural law, civil law, and public law) to an originary essence, that of the natural law of the originary subject: man in the state of nature.

Whereas Machiavelli thinks in the fact to be accomplished and the beginning, *natural law philosophy thinks in the accomplished fact and the origin*. The origin, which I am opposing to the beginning here, is obviously altogether different from the beginning. The origin is not the event in which the beginning of a form of eternity supervenes on the ground [*sur le fond*] of a matter that is already present, always already present, but formless or formed differently. The origin belongs to a completely different mode [*mode*] of philosophical reference, a completely different world [*monde*] of philosophical reference. What is the origin? It is *the manifestation of titles of legitimacy in the self-evidence of nature*: the titles of legitimacy of the truth as well as the titles of legitimacy of every essence and, in particular, the titles of legitimacy of the essence of civil law and the essence of public law.

Why is this so in natural law philosophy? For a simple reason which, obviously, would call for a great deal of explanation, but which we can begin to state as follows: because the idea of the origin that identifies the origin with nature and makes nature self-evident for a subject of law – because this idea of the origin, in the form I have indicated, was then, in the seventeenth and eighteenth centuries, the form par excellence of philosophical thought. These terms must be taken in the strong sense: the form par excellence of philosophical thought, that is, the form of foundation, the form of justification, the form of legitimization of philosophical thought, of philosophical thought as founding, justifying, legitimatizing. If, in this period, natural law theorists thought in the origin, it is because the origin was the philosophical form of legitimization of the titles of every essence, and because these theorists had to proceed by way of this common form to justify their own divergent political positions with regard to their common object, absolute monarchy, which had, accordingly, become their common philosophical problem.

So it was that the problem of absolute monarchy became for all of them, pro or con, the philosophical problem of the origin of the state, setting out from the state of origin, the state of nature, and natural law: the problem, the transition from the state of nature to the nature of the state, which was resolved, as you know, by the social contract. I shall go no further for now; I would simply like to say that, in moving from Machiavelli to Rousseau, we change worlds. As we just saw, we change the object of reflection and, simultaneously, we change the form of philosophical thought.

———

We know who Rousseau is. We know it officially, as it were. Why? Because he has been inscribed in the history of philosophy. And he has been inscribed in the history of philosophy by philosophy itself, which has thus inscribed him in its own history: for example, between Locke and Condillac on the one hand and Kant and Hegel on the other. Thus Rousseau occupies a well-defined place. This place has been accorded him on the basis of the observation of, and reflection on, a certain number of concepts which he put forward and which have been recognized as philosophy by the history of philosophy, by philosophy in its history: the concepts that Kant, for example, singled out in Rousseau.

I would like to try to show that, beyond this official recognition of Rousseau, this inscription of Rousseau in the history of philosophy, there exists an aspect of Rousseau, there exist words of Rousseau's and arguments of Rousseau's which, like Machiavelli's – this is why the comparison does not seem to me to be entirely arbitrary – have practically remained a dead letter. To put it differently, there exist words in Rousseau, and perhaps concepts and arguments as well, which were not registered by philosophy in its history when philosophy drew up the accounts of its history or settled its accounts with its own history. The philosophy that has inscribed Rousseau in its history for one or another merit has drawn up its accounts, and its tallies are accurate – but with the figures it has registered. The drawback, or the boon, is that a few figures, a few words, a few concepts have been left out of account, have been neglected. I would like to try to sketch not an exhaustive inventory of these Rousseauesque words and concepts left out of account by the history of philosophy, but an inventory of just a handful of them.

To this end, I shall be focusing my lectures on the second Discourse, the *Discourse on the Origin of Inequality among Men*. To pose the problem, I shall set out from the following aporia or contradiction. With Rousseau, we are quite obviously (since I've already discussed Machiavelli on the one hand and natural law philosophy on the other) in the same problematic and the same basic concepts as those of the whole natural law school, that is, the same concepts we have found in Hobbes and Locke.[3] There are doubtless differences between Rousseau, Hobbes, and Locke, but there were also differences between Locke and Hobbes, between Grotius and Pufendorf, between Burlamaqui and Locke; ultimately, the difference between Rousseau and his predecessors is no greater than the differences between his predecessors themselves. If we were able to speak of a thought common to his predecessors, we have to extend it to Rousseau as well: for the basis is plainly the same.

Let us put that more precisely. The form of thought which we see at work in Rousseau, and which commands everything, is the same form of thought as in his predecessors: it is the thought of the origin, the thought that has recourse to the origin. Rousseau very clearly says in several passages that we must go back to society's origins to expose its foundations, that there can be no other way: this way is mandatory for everyone. He adds that this origin is man's nature, man in the state of nature. He repeats, then, what his predecessors have said.

Here, for example, is a passage from the second Discourse: 'this . . . study of original man, of his true needs and the fundamental principle of his duties, is also the only effective means for doing away with the host of difficulties that present themselves regarding the origin of moral inequality, the true foundations of the body politic, the reciprocal rights of its members, and countless other similar matters whose importance is equalled only by their obscurity.'[4] Elsewhere, Rousseau writes: 'about [the state of nature]

3 Althusser's lectures on Machiavelli and Rousseau were preceded by four lectures on Hobbes and Locke delivered in October and November 1971.

4 Jean-Jacques Rousseau, *Discourse on the Origin of Inequality*, ed. Patrick Coleman, trans. Franklin Philip, Oxford: Oxford University Press, 2009, p. 18.

we should ... have accurate notions in order to judge our present state properly.'[5]

The procedure is thus perfectly clear. It is essential to go back to the state of nature, the state of origin, in order to discover man's nature there: only on this condition can we come to know natural right [*droit*], natural law [*loi*], the foundation of societies, civil law, political institutions, and the inequality that reigns among men in our present state. Thus the general form of philosophical discourse remains the same. And, in the general form of recourse to the origin, we see the same major categories of thought come into play in Rousseau as in all his predecessors, namely: the state of nature, the state of war, natural right, natural law, the social contract, sovereignty, civil law. This is the obligatory arsenal of this thought of the origin in the field of law.

These categories are grouped together under three basic moments of reflection that punctuate the manifestation of the essence of law. You know these three moments: the state of nature (the first moment), the social contract (the second moment), and the civil state (the third moment). In Rousseau, as in his predecessors, this originary genesis that sets out from the state of nature does not function like a historical genesis. Rather, in Rousseau, as in his predecessors, it functions like an analysis of essence grounded in the self-evidence of its original credentials, nature.

You may recall that Hobbes proposed to consider society as 'dissolved', as he puts it, in order to discern its original elements. Rousseau, for his part, calls on a different image: that of foundations buried in dust and sand. 'Human institutions', he writes, 'appear at first glance founded on shifting sands. It is only on closer examination, only after clearing away the dust and sand surrounding the edifice, that we perceive the unshakeable base on which it has been built and learn to respect its foundations.'[6] If we

5   Ibid., p. 15.
6   Ibid., pp. 18–19.

compare this image of the foundations, 'after clearing away the dust and sand', with several other passages in the second Discourse, in particular the famous lines in which Rousseau says that the state of nature may never have existed, it seems quite certain that, in Rousseau, the originary genesis is not a real genesis, a historical genesis, but is simply, as in his predecessors, an analysis of essence that takes the form of a genesis which is not historical, but theoretical. Why? In order to justify the determinations of this essence in its origin as the foundation of right.

There we have what strikes every reader of Rousseau. On this common ground, which leagues Rousseau with Hobbes, Locke, and the others, Rousseau is supposed, at best, to have elaborated certain variations of his own which distinguish him from his predecessors, yet are no more, in sum, than variations of one and the same invariant.[7] In opposition to this view, which can be defended, but which can also be criticized, I would simply like to suggest one idea, just one, and then I would like to attempt to analyse and demonstrate it.

Here is my idea: this similarity that we have just noted in our turn, that we have just acknowledged, this similarity in fact conceals a profound difference. It is not a difference in themes, motifs, or variations, not a difference affecting only a handful of concepts, but one that goes much deeper: *a difference in problematic and object*. I believe, and shall try to show, that the classic problematic that I have just recalled is in fact worked on [*travaillé*] in Rousseau, obscurely worked on, worked on in a way that appears on the edges of consciousness but is not always conscious, worked on by an essential difference, worked on by a divergence in viewpoint, a divergence in thought. Where is this work performed? At

---

7   The year 1970 saw the publication of Robert Derathé's magisterial *Jean-Jacques Rousseau et la science politique de son temps*. Derathé situates Rousseau with respect to received concepts and goes on to point out similarities and differences.

several very precise points, I believe. How is this work performed? That is what we are going to try to find out.

Here, in outline, is how I plan to proceed. We shall first discern this difference at work, in a radical, contradictory form, in connection with the concept of the origin itself. That will be the first part of my discussion. We shall then go on to observe all its effects unfolding along with the dispositive of the moments of the genesis which brings about the transition from the state of nature to the civil state. That will be the second part of my discussion. I think I shall limit myself to the first part today.

Here, then, is the first part of this attempt at a demonstration. I shall call it *the circle of the origin*. What makes Rousseau resemble all the natural law philosophers is the fact that he thinks in the origin, as they do. We have established this once and for all and shall not go back to it. Yet what distinguishes Rousseau from them, radically, is that he is the only philosopher of the origin, the only one of all the natural law philosophers who think in the origin, *to think the concept of the origin in its own right* – to think it in the strong sense, that is, not just to use it, practise it, manipulate it, wield it, not just to think *in* the concept, but to think the concept in the strong sense, to confront it as an object, to confront the origin as object, to make it an object in order to think it, think it in the form of a concept. Of all the natural law philosophers, Rousseau is, then, the only one to do this, to think the concept of the origin as such. He is also the only one to propose, in one and the same movement of thought, a radical critique of it.

Here are the two passages of the second Discourse which are crucial in this regard. They occur at the beginning of the second Discourse.[8]

---

8   TN: Only the latter of these two passages occurs near the beginning of the

'I have dwelt so long on the hypothesis of this [state of nature] (here is the crucial passage) because, having to overcome age-old errors and entrenched beliefs, I thought it necessary to dig down to the roots.'[9] First passage.

Second passage: 'Philosophers examining the foundations of society [that is, the natural law philosophers] have all felt the need to go back to the state of nature, but not one of them has managed to reach it.'[10]

I believe that, if we take these two affirmations of Rousseau's seriously, we can already see a certain difference emerging. Rousseau affirms that he has had to combat 'age-old errors and entrenched beliefs', and these 'age-old errors and entrenched beliefs' are, precisely, the errors and beliefs of his predecessors from the natural law school – Hobbes's and Locke's errors, as we shall see.

Rousseau declares that those philosophers have clearly felt 'the need to go back to the state of nature, but not one of them has managed to reach it'. If they have not, it is because they are stuck fast in 'age-old errors'. As for him – he is the only one to have done this – he has resolved to go further, to go all the way; he has had 'to dig down to the roots' to get past the stage of 'age-old errors'. For these 'roots' are the stage, the endpoint, that the philosophers, all the philosophers, have been unable to reach or not known how to reach. None of them has ever arrived at the state of nature. This sentence is rather stupefying, after all. Here, then, is the first contradiction. It is necessary to go back to the state of nature; all have felt that, yet no one has ever succeeded in doing it.

What does this contradiction mean? What does this sentence mean? What is the status of this contradiction? In what sense is there a contradiction? How can it be thought? Is it a subjective

---

second Discourse. The former is similar to a passage that occurs there (Rousseau, *Discourse on the Origin of Inequality*, p. 18).

9   Ibid., p. 51.
10   Ibid., p. 24.

contradiction or an objective contradiction? A contingent contradiction or a necessary contradiction? What do these contradictory sentences refer us to? To answer these questions, we have to examine the examples that Rousseau adduces. In other words, we have to examine what Rousseau thinks of his predecessors, who, stuck fast in 'age-old errors', did not succeed in reaching the state of nature, although they sensed that one had to go all the way back to it.

We shall therefore have to examine the case of the natural law philosophers. We shall be obliged, therefore, to take on the task of examining what Rousseau denounces as the circle of their theory. First point, then: the theorists' circle. The theorists are, basically, Hobbes, Locke, and all the other natural law philosophers.

In Rousseau's view, these philosophers failed to reach the state of nature: they got stuck in errors en route. Why? Because they perpetrated a circle. What does this circle consist in? Immediately after the lines I just cited, about the philosophers who felt the need to go back to the state of nature, yet failed to reach it, Rousseau defines their mistake. Their mistake is that they never ceased presupposing what was in question. For example: 'Some have not hesitated to assume that man in that state [the state of nature] possessed a notion of the just and unjust [this applies to Locke], without bothering to show that he must have had such a concept or that he would even find it useful.'[11] Another quotation: 'Others begin by giving [that is, by giving from the outset, hence in the state of nature] the strongest persons authority over the weaker ones, and straightaway [that is, from the state of nature on] introduced government without thinking of the time that had to elapse before the words "authority" and "government" could have any meaning for men.'[12] (This is probably an allusion to Grotius.)

11 Ibid.
12 Ibid.

Consequently, and this can be generalized, all these theorists supposed, that is, presupposed, that men in the state of nature had qualities, meanings, and significations which could in fact only come about under other conditions, long after the state of nature, in the civil state.

Let us spell out the meaning of this supposition, this presupposition. We can immediately take the example of Hobbes. Here is what Rousseau writes:

> Hobbes clearly saw the flaw in all modern definitions of natural right [that is, moral definitions, which is what Rousseau has in mind here], but the conclusions he drew from his own definition show that his own concept of natural right is no less false . . . He introduc[ed] into savage man's concern for his own survival the need to satisfy a host of passions that are the handiwork of society.[13]

That is, Hobbes ascribes what is a result of the history of social life to the state of nature.

Another example: Locke, whom Rousseau discusses under the same general heading as Hobbes in Note L to the second Discourse; he discusses them together. 'Locke's argument thus collapses, and all his dialectic has not saved him from the error committed by Hobbes and others. They had to explain a fact about the state of nature . . . and it did not occur to these philosophers to look back across the centuries of society.'[14] That is, they remained in present-day society. And here is the argument that sums up all the others, that sums up this process in both senses of the word: the theorists' thought process [*procès*] and the trial [*procès*] Rousseau subjects them to. Here is the sentence: 'All these philosophers . . . have imported into the state of nature ideas they had

---

13 Ibid., p. 44.
14 Ibid., pp. 113–14.

taken from society. They talk of savage man and they depict civilized man.'[15]

The essence of the mistake of the philosophers of the state of nature thus consists in a supposition, which is itself a presupposition, which is itself a transference, a retrospective projection of the civil state (the present state of civil man, man as formed by society and history) onto the state of nature and natural man, both supposed to exist before history. As it operates in the theorists, recourse to the state of nature therefore appears as a circle. It is a circle from the standpoint of its determinations, since the state of nature is thought in the determinations of the civil state, since the theorists attribute to the man of the state of nature determinations which are meaningful only in society and can only be the determinations, passions, attributes, and faculties of men of the civil state (for example, reason, self-esteem, and so on).

This circle of the theorists is a circle from the standpoint of the *form* of thought, since the result – that is, the social state, the civil state – is projected onto the origin the better to produce the result, when the result has in fact already been projected onto, has already been presupposed in, the form of its origin. Thus the result very easily becomes the cause of itself, the legitimization of itself in the guise of the origin, since we have to do with nothing but a repetition here. The result exists in two forms: in the form of the result in civil society and in the form of the same result, but in the state of nature. The objective, function, and effect of this transposition is, quite simply, to legitimize what exists in the state of society by transposing its results to the state of nature, the state of origin.

It is impossible to say more forthrightly than Rousseau does that recourse to the origin is merely a veiled form of justifying what is, in the full sense of the word. Recourse to the origin is not just in the reactionary sense, if you like, but also in the most general sense, merely a veiled form of the justification of what is, whether

---

15   Ibid., p. 24.

it is the existing social state of the accomplished fact or the social state that one desires. In other words, Rousseau here sketches not just a critique of the justification of the accomplished fact, the reigning order, but also a critique of the utopianism that hopes to justify the future of the society it desires by projecting it onto the origins, by grounding it in the origins. Rousseau affirms: 'writers begin by searching for the rules on which it would be appropriate for men to agree for the common welfare; and then they give the name "natural law" to this collection of rules';[16] and, naturally, natural law is projected onto the state of nature, onto the origin, which provides it with its foundations. For example – a different example this time, an apologist for the accomplished fact, Grotius, targeted in chapter 2 of book 1 of *The Social Contract* – as much sovereignty and submission is projected onto the state of nature as is needed to subject men in civil life to a king. A master–slave relationship is created in the state of nature which, when it is trans- posed to the civil state, makes it possible to justify the accomplished fact of absolute monarchy.

Let us leave the political and polemical applications of Rous- seau's thesis to one side. They call into question the political choices of the theorists of absolute monarchy in both its dictatorial phase – that is, Hobbes – and its liberal phase – that is, Locke. More generally, these theses of Rousseau's call the idealism of Enlighten- ment philosophy into question, for what is Enlightenment philosophy? Rousseau discusses it in connection with philoso- phers in general, and he also discusses it in connection with Diderot. What is Enlightenment philosophy, if not the projection of the end [*fin*] of history, namely, reason, onto the origin? What matters for us, beyond these polemical objectives, is the theor- etical significance of Rousseau's critique of recourse to the origin.

For the first time, a philosopher who openly thinks in the origin faces up to the task of thinking the origin in its concept,

16   Ibid., p. 17.

and does so in order to denounce it in the guise of what we shall now call *the false origin*. In the process, however, Rousseau well and truly produces a critique of the concept of the origin. Recourse to the origin is denounced as a circular, speculary operation that comes into contradiction with its declared function. Philosophers rightly felt the need to have recourse to the state of nature and the state of origin, and to aspire to attain the true origin (which should make it possible to grasp the truth at its birth and in its nakedness), but they failed to arrive at the true state of nature, the true origin; they reached only a false origin. This false origin, that of the theorists and philosophers, is an imposture, because it is merely a transference of the result itself back onto the origin, because it is the imposture of the result *declared to be the origin*. This transference is not a simple mistake, the effect of which would be a sort of philosophical rubbish that is nil or negligible. Quite the contrary: it must be said that the reality of this transference, hence the reality of the false origin (Rousseau sketches a theory of it), is its function; it is the justification of the order one desires to see reign, or the justification of the reigning order, namely, the king.

But that is not all. Beneath this condemnation of the false origin, of its structure and function, we discover that its meaning is not quite the one we originally thought, that of being a purely theoretical genesis, a pure analysis of essence utterly foreign to a historical genesis. We discover that the political and theoretical function of recourse to the origin brings it into relation with real history, with the historical present, with our present state, in which theorists stage recourse to an ahistorical origin for reasons that are mandated by the present and are, consequently, historical through and through. Thus something comes into view behind this radical refutation, something that Rousseau necessarily takes into account, must necessarily take into account (in a certain way that has not yet been defined) and take seriously, something that must be called, provisionally, *history*.

We shall not, however, stop with the theorists' circle in our reading of Rousseau; we shall go beyond this object to discuss another which accounts for it. That is to say – and this will be the second moment of our examination – we shall discover the reason for the theorists' circle in the circle of denaturation or the circle of alienation.

The theorists' circle is not a subjective aberration. It possesses an objective rationality. Thinking in the false origin is never anything but justification in thought for what is politically desirable or what exists. Rousseau, however, does not remain at the level of what could become a political psychologism. He asks the following question, or allows us to ask it, or compels us to ask it: Why does the theorists' thinking necessarily take the form of a circle? Why are the theorists condemned to the false origin?

Rousseau answers: because they are subject to another circle that is not theoretical, but real – a universal circle, because they are themselves caught in, inscribed in, a universal circle from which they cannot escape. This circle is that of present-day, denatured, alienated society. Ultimately, it is the very essence of present-day society that is reflected in the theorists' powerlessness to leave this circle, and in the fact that they repeat, in thought, this circle which society draws around them.

In other words, at the very moment when Rousseau might seem to succumb to the subjectivism of a political psychology, he eludes it. The theorists' circle is not in their political will; rather, it is at the very basis of their political consciousness and in their theoretical consciousness, merely the realization and repetition of a completely different circle, which simultaneously dominates politics as well as its theoretical justification: the circle of man's and present-day society's social denaturation and social alien-ation. Why, ultimately, have the theorists proven unable to go back to the state of nature? Basically, because it is lost. Because nature is lost. Because there is no more nature. One can almost say that. I say 'almost', and we shall see why. *There is no more nature.*

The theorists' mistake accordingly becomes, when it is thus referred to its ultimate condition, something like a pre-Kantian transcendental mistake, a mistake that is in some sense inevitable in the human condition. There is no lack of texts by Rousseau on this point. He asks why 'it is no small undertaking to separate what is inborn from what is artificial in the present nature of man'.[17] 'How will man come to see himself as nature created him, through all the changes that must have been produced in his original constitution in the course of time and events, and how can we separate what he owes to his inborn resources from what circumstances and his advances have added to or changed in his primitive state?'[18] He asks why 'Diogenes could not find a man', if not 'because he searched among his contemporaries for a man from a time that no longer was'?[19] Why do we find all these repeated questions in Rousseau, if not because, as he writes, the 'paths that must have led man from the natural state to the civil state' have been 'lost and forgotten'? Because, he says, 'man has changed [his] nature'. Because, he says, 'original man [has] disappeared'.[20] Because, as he puts it in a fragment titled 'State of War', nature has 'disappeared every-where';[21] or, again, because reason has 'smother[ed] nature'.[22]

On this theme of a vanished, lost, smothered nature, we should refer to the most dramatic passage, which is at the same time the most accurate from the theoretical point of view: the passage at the beginning of the second Discourse in which the image of Glaucus appears. Here it is:

---

17   Ibid., p. 15.
18   Ibid., p. 14.
19   Ibid., p. 83.
20   Ibid.
21   Rousseau, 'L'État de guerre', in *The Political Writings*, ed. Charles E. Vaughan, vol. 1, Cambridge: Cambridge University Press, 1915, p. 296.
22   Rousseau, *Discourse on the Origin of Inequality*, p. 18.

Like the statue of Glaucus so disfigured by time, the sea, and
storms as to look less like a god than a wild beast, the human
soul modified in society by innumerable constantly recurring
causes – the acquisition of a mass of knowledge and a multitude
of errors, changes that took place in the constitution of the
body, the constant onslaught of the passions – has, as it were, so
changed its appearance as to be nearly unrecognizable.[23]

Nature has one last chance; we shall see why. Let us simply note,
in light of the handful of indications offered by the texts just cited,
the reason for the loss and forgetting of nature. Why is nature lost,
why is it forgotten? Why is there no more nature? This loss and
forgetting are not sanctioned by the void and nothingness. If
nature is lost, it is because we can no longer find it, find it in person.
If nature is forgotten, it is because we can no longer recall it or call
it back. In fact, nature is present, but in its loss and forgetting, in
the form of loss and the form of forgetting. This form of loss and
forgetting is the form of a cover-up [*recouvrement*]. Nature is
covered over by the whole history of its modifications, by all the
effects of its history. It is 'disfigured' – the word is Rousseau's – by
the whole history of its progress. It is, in a word – this is Rousseau's
key word – 'denatured' by the whole history of the loss of its
nature. This is a term that we can translate into a terminology
more familiar to us by saying that *nature is alienated, that it no
longer exists except in the other-than-itself*, in its contrary, the social
passions, and even in reason subject to the social passions. In short,
nature is alienated in its real history, and the result of this alienation holds sway over the present-day world and the theorists who
go looking for this lost origin.

Third point: after the circle of social alienation, the circle of the
human sciences. I did not speak about the theorists by accident a
moment ago. It is in setting out from this circle that we can find

23   Ibid., p. 14.

our way back to the natural law theorists' mistake and, in general, to the sciences that promise knowledge of man. Rousseau discusses them under the name of 'sciences'. It is not a question of mathematics. In question are, basically, the sciences that make it possible for us to know man, or ought to. Do these sciences not make it possible to leave the circle of alienation? The human sciences are not just caught in the circle of alienation; they are, in some sort, the higher form and ruse of this alienation, those that imagine they can escape it: 'Since all the advances of the human race continually move it ever further from its primitive state', Rousseau writes, 'the more new knowledge we accumulate, the more we deprive ourselves of the means for acquiring the most important knowledge of all. Thus, in a sense, it is by studying man that we have made ourselves incapable of knowing him.'[24]

Why 'incapable of knowing him'? Because scientific books, far from acquainting us with original man, merely teach us, says Rousseau, to see men 'as they have made themselves';[25] that is to say, the result again. This cause, however, is itself but an effect. It is not just the present-day object of the sciences that is denatured – men as they have made themselves. It is not just their present-day object that denatures the sciences, but their scientific nature as such, in so far as it is produced by exercising reason. Because reason is at work in the sciences, the sciences cannot but be denatured.

Unlike the philosophes, Rousseau has not projected reason onto the state of nature. Reason is not an originary faculty; Rousseau does not presuppose reason in the natural individual. On the contrary, he shows that reason is a product of human history, that it makes its appearance in the course of human history, and that its development is organically bound up with the development of the social passions on which it depends. The upshot is that reason cannot be pure; the upshot is that the maturation of

24   Ibid.
25   Ibid., p. 17.

reason in man coincides with man's denaturation. The human sciences are therefore themselves trapped in covering-over, forgetting, denaturation: they belong to the genesis of denaturation. By definition, every human science is a forgetting of the origin, not just because it has lost what Rousseau calls the 'pure movement' 'prior to all reflection,'[26] but also because it has never been in a position to lose it, since it is a product of reason, since it was itself born of the loss of the origin. Science thus is, in a certain way, absolute forgetting, because it has been caught up, from its birth, in the forgetting that constituted it, because it was born only at a certain point in the process of the constitution of forgetting, in the process of the constitution of denaturation. The sciences accordingly belong to the circle of alienation by virtue not just of their object, but also of their essence, which inscribes them in denaturation, that is, in the lost origin.

Thus we have come back to our starting point. If the theorists have recourse to the false origin, this is not just an effect of their pure political subjectivity. In their circle, they simply reproduce, in the form of theoretical arguments expressing their political choices, the circle of the sciences and, more generally, that of reason, which is, in the last instance, the circle of the alienation of men from society. Thus we see the theorists' arguments, their reason and their concepts, going round and round in the philosophical circle of the projection of the result onto its origin. They go round and round in theory, however, only because they cannot but go round and round in the circle of denaturation, of alienation. They cannot but go round and round there.

Why? Because their search for the origin is futile, because the origin is lost, because the human world itself has confined itself in its result, in generalized alienation and denaturation, and because the theorists cannot leave the circle of this objective result. The proof is that, when they think they have found the origin, they

---

26 Ibid., p. 46.

never find anything but the result again. This for two reasons: nature is absent from the circle; and reason cannot leave the circle because it belongs to it.

Let us take a break here, if you don't mind.

Faced with this theory of the circle of the bad origin and what analysis of it has showed us, namely, the circle of human reason and, in the last instance, the circle of the alienation and denaturation of human history, we could give two possible interpretations. I shall present them to you schematically, in a few words.

On the first interpretation, which a Kantian might defend, only two terms would be singled out for attention in what has just been evoked: first, the circle of recourse to the origin and, second, the circle of reason. The circle of historical alienation would be left aside. On that condition, one could say that what is manifested in the circle of the origin is the circle of reason, and go on to argue that there is something like an anticipation of a transcendental theory of error in Rousseau. One could call this theory transcendental, because this error of reason is a necessary error: it is the necessary error of reason trying to go beyond its own limits. One could also call this theory transcendental because the content and form of this error could be put down to the paralogism of recourse to the origin. That is, recourse to the origin could be thought as a paralogism, as a result thought as its own origin – that is, as a paralogism of the unconditioned. Thus a Kantian could appropriate Rousseau's argument in order to defend the idea that Rousseau anticipates a transcendental theory of error. However, if it is to be sustained, this interpretation obviously must, as I said, leave another term to one side, the third term: the alienation of human history.

If, now, we reintroduce this third term, we have three terms: we have recourse to the origin, we have the circle of reason, and we have the circle of alienation. If we take these three terms seriously, we can defend another interpretation. We can defend the idea that

Rousseau presents us with two things: first, a general theory of the human sciences' political determination, or the human sciences' political dependency on the human and political world. The sciences are determined by the human and political world, and this political dependency of the human sciences takes a very precise form: that is, the human and political world in existence today reflects its own objectives in the human sciences in the form of these human sciences' objects. To put it differently, the human sciences reflect, in the form of their objects, the political objectives of the world that determines them. Completely determined by this human world of denaturation and alienation, they have no object other than its objectives, reflected in them in the form of objects.

This is the first theory that Rousseau might be said to offer us in this conceptual ensemble. He might be said to offer us something else again. He might be said simultaneously to offer us a *general theory of philosophical mystification*, a general theory of philosophy in which philosophy would intervene simply in order to provide the established order or social reformers' political projects with illusory theoretical credentials [*titres de validité*] – necessarily illusory, but socially necessary. On this reading, philosophy intervenes as a socially necessary mystification of thought by way of the origin; it intervenes as thought that functions at the origin in order to provide the established order or projects of social reform with illusory, yet socially necessary, credentials. There we have the second fairly coherent interpretation that might be formulated at the point we have reached.

However, we obviously must, in order to confer a certain coherency on this second hypothesis, leave aside the question as to how Rousseau, the individual named Rousseau, trapped in the social dependency that he himself discusses, can nevertheless pronounce a discourse on dependency. What is the status of Rousseau's discourse with respect to his own general theory of the status of any possible discourse? How can Rousseau utter this discourse, if not because he himself has access to the true origin? At the same time, if this second interpretation is to hold up, we must leave the following question aside: How can knowledge of the true origin also escape philosophical mystification?

In other words, one asks the same question twice. How is it that Rousseau can escape the circles: firstly, the circle of society and the determination of every science by society; secondly, the circle of recourse to the origin, the circle of philosophical reason? How is it that Rousseau can escape these two circles? The fact is that he does, because he discusses them. By what right can he discuss them, if not because he has escaped them? If he has escaped them, how was he able to state the theory of the impossibility of escaping them?

In other words, we fall into the trap of what must now be called – fourth point – *Rousseau's circle*. To try to extricate ourselves from this situation of the street-car in motion that goes nowhere, in which we have just spent a moment or two, we have exactly to recall the results we have attained; that is, we have to put our question in precise form. What is Rousseau's position, what can Rousseau's position be, after this radical denunciation of thinking by way of the origin? There we have the terms of the problem as they should be precisely summed up.

Firstly, it is imperative to go back to the origin (Rousseau thinks in the origin, no doubt about it), as the theorists have well understood. Secondly, it is necessary radically to reject the false origin that they have not been able to go beyond; they are caught in the stranglehold of a necessity that goes beyond them, they have been locked into a circle that he has gone beyond, since it was a circle that encompassed both human society and human reason: the circle of human denaturation, of human alienation. It follows, thirdly, that if it is necessary to go back to the origin, and if it is necessary radically to reject the false origin, one has to think a completely different origin, the true one, and gain access to it by completely different means, avoiding the trap of philosophical reason (since we have seen that there is an essential complicity between the false origin and the theoretical means that the philosophers employed in order to think it).

It is, then, necessary to think a completely different origin and gain access to it by completely different means. A completely different origin: that is, a state of nature, since it is necessary to go back to the state of nature, but one which cannot have, as its contents, a projection of the present social state, and which will not instate the result of the origin as the origin of the origin. And it will be necessary to gain access to the origin by means completely different from reason; no longer, that is, by means of ratiocinative reason [*raison raisonnante*], but by means of a different faculty, a different power.

The question that arises at the point we have now reached is obviously whether this undertaking is at all possible. In fact, for Rousseau, the question has already been resolved. To be able to utter the discourse which brings the circle of the theorists of the origin into relation with the alienation of reason and human society, and, quite simply, to be able to write, to pronounce, to utter the simple little word '*denaturation*', to be able to construct the whole general theory that depends on it and commands the critique based on the theory of the bad origin, Rousseau himself must already be in nature and the good origin. It is obvious that he cannot utter all these discourses unless he already is in nature.

What matters to us is to know how he can be in nature and the good origin, to discover the path on which he is able to reach it. In other words, what matters to us is that his written theory, the theory written by Rousseau, authorizes this situation attained by Rousseau, this exceptional situation – that is, authorizes this solution, in other words, the fact that what is a solution for Rousseau is, for us, a problem that can be given this solution. It seemed to me that that was spelled out in his text, and the fact is that it is. The theory of denaturation and alienation – let me make it clear that the word 'alienation' in the sense in which I am using it is not Rousseau's, only the word 'denaturation' is truly his – this

theory of denaturation is not a theory of complete, absolute denaturation. It maintains rare ways out, narrow ways out, but it does
maintain them. We might cite the text about Glaucus again: 'the
human soul has, as it were, so changed its appearance as to be nearly
unrecognizable.' This 'nearly unrecognizable', this nearly nothing,
suffices to allow recognition of the unrecognizable, because it is
only nearly unrecognizable, not absolutely unrecognizable.

This means that, under certain conditions and, above all, on the
radical precondition of the critique of the false origin, it is possible
to gain access to the true origin, to knowledge of natural man. This
operation supposes a radical modification in both the object and
the subject. 'Radical modification': those are not words tossed off
lightly; 'radical modification' means that Rousseau must propose
altogether novel solutions, solutions unprecedented in the history
of natural law, unprecedented in both his predecessors and his
contemporaries. And that is just what he does: he proposes such
solutions.

In the object, Rousseau produces – that is to say, writes, puts
down in writing, advances, thinks, reasons by means of, produces,
advances – Rousseau advances a concept that is absolutely without
precedent in the entire history of natural law philosophy. It is the
decisive concept in the second Discourse. I mention it now; I shall
have occasion to come back to it. It is the concept of the *state of
pure nature*; not the state of nature, but the state of *pure* nature. We
shall have occasion to discuss it. Here it is enough to know that
this state of pure nature represents the 'roots' that Rousseau talks
about: 'down to the roots', 'dig down to the roots', one has to go
that far, and it is that far that Rousseau has gone and that the
others were not capable of going; it is the point that the philosophers proved unable to reach when they wanted to have recourse
to the state of nature, the point that Rousseau alone has proved
capable of seeing, conceiving of, and stating, that of which he has
provided the concept. In fact – and we can judge this by its results,
which are considerable – it is the point on which everything is

decided between the false origin and the true origin, the point or the radical line of demarcation; it is the 'roots', it is the state of pure nature. So much for the object.

As for the subject, albeit trapped in social denaturation and theoretical alienation, it must be in a position to accede to this concept of pure nature. Now we know what must be grasped by the subject, hence by any subject whatsoever, hence by Rousseau, hence by you and me: the state of pure nature. In the subject, then, one has to bring out, one has to produce, a new means that will make it possible to grasp this new object. Rousseau produces something novel here as well, something new, a faculty corresponding specifically to this discovery: no longer reason, but the *heart*.

Of course, the heart is better known than the state of pure nature, but we have to take due note of it anyway. What is the heart? The heart is direct, immediate access to nature; but, practically speaking, with respect to the problem to hand, it is the way out of the circle of ratiocinative reason. As Rousseau puts it, in fragments for which I have the references that I can give you: 'The state of society, which imposes constraints on our natural inclinations, is nevertheless not capable of doing away with them; despite our prejudices and despite us, they continue to speak in the depth of our heart.' Something still speaks in the depth of our hearts (this comes from a treatise on 'The State of War').[27] 'I have therefore abandoned reason and consulted nature, that is, the inner sentiment that governs my belief independently of my reason.'[28] All these words are very important and call for comment. 'I have abandoned reason and consulted nature': that is, nature = an 'inner sentiment that directs my belief independently of my reason'. In another letter, Rousseau writes: 'this sentiment is that of nature itself', and so on.

---

27   Rousseau, 'L'État de guerre', p. 305.
28   Jean-Jacques Rousseau, Letter to Jacob Vernes, 18 February 1758, in Rousseau, *Lettres philosophiques*, Paris: Livre de Poche, 2003, p. 175.

As far as the heart goes, there is, if you like, an entire literature on Rousseau and the heart, and so on. What interests us here is the theoretical significance of this faculty, this power; what interests us is to find out how it functions. It does not at all function in the mode of the heart; it is in fact an extremely precise faculty whose concept can be provided. In other words, the heart is not grasped by the heart; the heart can perfectly well be thought, because the essential feature of the heart in Rousseau is that it is *a heart which thinks*. It is a heart which guides reason, which directs reason. Formally, as we have just brought it into play here, the heart, the intervention of the heart, does not extricate us from the structure of thought by way of the origin, since it reproduces the dominant philosophical scheme of nature. It is nature as a form of manifestation of the rightful credentials of the essence in its self-evidence. Nature is what is visible, what is heard, and so on. That does not make for a radical change in the form of philosophical thought, since the theory of the heart in Rousseau reproduces the form of the originary subjectivity to which this originary nature is given as self-evident. This nature that is the originary self-evidence of the rightful credentials of every essence is originarily given as self-evident to an originary subjectivity that grasps it as such in its self-evident immediacy and its transparency and its very presence. This is, for example, the status of the Cartesian subject of the *ego cogito*, the status of the subject of eighteenth-century psychological empiricism, and so on. It is exactly the heart's status in Rousseau: nature is transparency in its self-evidence.

Simply, what changes with the intervention of the heart in Rousseau is the name of this subjectivity. It is no longer reason, as was the case in the seventeenth and even the early eighteenth century; hence it is no longer the understanding, but the heart. What changes, in other words, is the form of manifestation of the originary self-evidence. I shall say that it is no longer light, but the voice. I am alluding to natural light: that is, nature is its own light, is itself light for consciousness, for the subject that will grasp

it, for the originary subject that will grasp it, and so on. Reason is
natural light, then, whereas Rousseau invokes the voice of nature,
which is to say that *self-evidence is that of a voice*. It is no longer that
of light and a gaze, but that of a voice and an ear.

Thus we shift from the identity of nature and reason in the form
of light to another identity: the identity of nature and the heart in
the form of the voice. Formally, then, we have the same structure of
interiority, but we witness a displacement inside this structure
of interiority, a displacement from reason to the heart and from
light to the voice. This displacement from reason to the heart and
from light to the voice is not the transition from one order to
another that is independent of the first, as if the philosophers – in
this case, Rousseau – had a series of pre-existing, independent
concepts at their disposal in some speculative world, and could
choose among them as need dictates. This displacement from
reason to the heart and from light to the voice is a displacement
that is determined not by Rousseau's choices – I would like to try
to show this – but by the concepts with regard to which this
displacement is effected, against which Rousseau marks out his
own position [*se démarque*]. This displacement is determined, in
other words, by the concepts of reason and light. It is with regard
to them that this displacement is carried out; they are the concepts
that determine this displacement.

To put it differently, the heart and the voice do not have a
meaning that is theirs by some inherent right. They do not have
referents or correspond to external realities; their meaning is
wholly internal to the world of philosophy. They take their philosophical meaning not from philosophical objects, but from
their philosophical intervention. That is, the heart and the voice
take their philosophical meaning from the determinate distance
that they carve between themselves – they are what intervenes –
and the concepts which (this is their effect) they drive to the
back of the philosophical stage: the old concepts of reason
and light.

The voice and the heart, however, do not have referents either, that is to say, are not the signifiers of objective signifieds any more than reason and light were. They are simply the philosophical mark of a philosophical demarcation, that is, of a critical distance taken from reason and light. This critical distance taken from reason and light is already crucial, because, for Rousseau, squarely in the middle of the eighteenth century, it signifies a demarcation from every existing construction of reason, from the idealism of reason, from reforming reason, from the philosophy of light and the philosophy of the Enlightenment. Heart and voice thus signify a rejection of all the theories of the bad origin and, at the same time, the announcement of a theory of the good origin by way of an appeal to the heart, the sensitive nature of the heart, and so on. In other words, voice and heart, demarcated in this way from reason and light, are now another name for another form of presence, different from that of light and reason. This other form of presence has, however, its own efficacity. It produces a double effect.

For one thing, it makes lost nature immediately present in this denatured human world, for nature still speaks in the depth of the heart, and does so here and now, in the present. For another, it makes it possible to free oneself from the antinomies of the circle of denaturation and the circle of reason. For recourse to the heart, this transition, this demarcation, this intervention of the heart and the voice bring off the impossible feat of leaving the absolutely closed circle of denaturation. They bring off the impossible feat of escaping from the circle without leaving it – since one cannot leave it – by, quite simply, going back into the self to find, in the heart, nature outside the circle, which continues to speak in the heart. It is an escape by way of the inside; *one leaves the circle by way of the inside*. It is, then, to leave the circle and reach, beyond the whole history of denaturation, nature in its first state, the pure state of nature. Not to leave the circle, but, instead of leaving the circle, which is impossible, to go back into the self and, by way of this inner escape, to find the origin again: that is, to enter into contact with the object which is the object of the pure state of nature.

For the heart has a content, an object – the one I have discussed, the pure state of nature. It is here that the determination of the object through demarcation culminates, for, while the intervention of heart and voice is determined by their demarcation from reason and light, this intervention is not merely critical. At the same time, it has the effect of constituting a new philosophical object, which is likewise demarcated from the preceding object and will be the object of the heart and the voice: this object is, precisely, the true origin; is, precisely, the pure state of nature, which is absent from the philosophy of reason and light.

To sum up this whole argument, which was no doubt abstract and in any case heavy going, I would like to say the following. Throughout this philosophical operation, which turns on the intervention of the heart, the important thing is to see that we cannot think the significance of the intervention of the heart in Rousseau unless that intervention is correlated with the object of the heart, with that to which the heart is referred as to its correlate. That said, when we observe the phenomenon of philosophical substitution that is carried out under the unity of the self-evidence of nature, which replaces reason and light with heart and voice, we have to do with the three following moments:

Firstly, we have to do with a displacement in the self-evidence of nature, one that brings about the transition from the pair reason–light to the pair heart–voice. The form in which nature is given as self-evident to an originary subject is no longer the pair reason–light, no longer the light of reason, no longer reason as light; it is the heart as voice, it is the voice of the heart, it is the voice of nature, and so on. This is, then, the first displacement.

[Secondly,] this displacement is in fact a determinate demarcation that distantiates the old forms of philosophical thought in order to impose the new ones; it has meaning only in this distantiation. It is in relation to these distantiated old forms of thought, that is, reason–light, that heart–voice appear in the foreground and function correlatively; function, that is, as a repelling couple vis-à-vis the forms they drive to the back of the philosophical stage.

Thirdly, this demarcation between forms – the forms, be it recalled, of reason–light on the one hand and heart–voice on the other, and so on – has a stake which is not just the forms themselves, but a new philosophical object. By philosophical object, I mean an object internal to philosophy, a philosophical object that will take the place of the old philosophical object. This new philosophical object is the true origin, which will replace the false origin. More precisely, in a determinate way as far as our reflection is concerned, the state of pure nature will replace the state of nature as it appears in Hobbes or Locke. Indeed, Rousseau has the impression of – not only has the impression of, but concretely produces the impression of – not only produces the impression of, but concretely produces – original forms of thought and original objects. This is attested by, among other things, the fact that he is conscious of it, and will consciously think this object's originality, as we shall see next time.

LECTURE TWO

3 March 1972

L AST TIME, WE STOPPED at a precise point, the intervention of the heart. I put forward the hypothesis that, in the second Discourse, the heart has an object, and that this object has a name; Rousseau calls it 'the pure state of nature' or 'the first state of nature'. I also told you that it was an object different from that of natural law philosophy.

Just as Rousseau tries to put another origin in place, to think another origin, so he produces another object corresponding to it. This object is, necessarily, an object that is thought. This object too will be thought by reflection and reasoning – in short, in the forms of the understanding, which means that recourse to the heart has nothing to do, in Rousseau, with an appeal to mystical feeling or the confusion of the *Schwärmerei* that Hegel was to condemn as the loss of philosophy and the loss of reason. What Rousseau calls for through the appeal to the heart is, in the quest for the good origin, the exercise of reason under the guidance of the heart; it is not the exclusion of reason, but the exercise of well-guided reason, well-guided under the guidance of the heart. More precisely, it is the exercise of reasoning and reflection in accordance with the principles of the heart, not vague, general principles, but extremely precise, extremely well-defined principles, those that are inscribed in the pure state of nature.

This allows us to declare the following two propositions equivalent: making the heart the first principle of reason is exactly the same as making the pure state of nature the first principle of the state of nature. I believe it can be shown that this division of the object into the object and the faculties is inscribed in the division of the concepts and the division of the text of Rousseau's second Discourse. For, when we consider the place that the discourse on pure nature occupies in Rousseau's text, we are struck by two traits.

This discourse stands, of course, at the beginning of the Discourse, because it is its first principle. At the same time, however, this discourse on the pure state of nature is, theoretically speaking, completely separate from the rest. This pure state of nature is an altogether unique state, because, without the natural accidents which eventually supervene – the cosmic accidents which overturn both the earth and the rhythm of nature, which modify the rhythm of the seasons, and so on – the state of pure nature would have remained in its pure state, that is, would have remained unchanged, endlessly repeating itself. This isolation is therefore a theoretical isolation that concerns not just the contents of the state of nature, but also its mode of existence and positing. For the state of pure nature is the origin itself, isolated as such, posited and thought as such. Its isolation is its purity made visible, made manifest. It is proof that the true origin has indeed been reached, since one can isolate it, at once in itself and from the rest, and since one can thus enable it to escape the fate of the false origin, which is the circle of the result cast back onto the origin.

This true origin is also isolated in another sense that is very important for us. After the pages of pure description that are devoted to it, in which Rousseau's philosophical thought functions by 'setting aside all the facts',[1] as he puts it, we see a form of reflection different from pure a priori deduction come into play, one that operates to define the state of pure nature. We see another form of reflection come into play: observation of the facts, combined in its turn with what Rousseau calls historical conjectures and hypotheses.[2] That is, we see two forms of reasoning at work in the second Discourse:

- a purely abstract form, deduction, which bears on the state of pure nature;
- and another form that is partly concrete and partly hypothetical, which bears on observation of the facts, which combines them with conjectures and hypotheses, and concerns everything else.

This very sharp separation brings out the fact that while it is reason which is at work in the exposition of the later genesis, observing and reflecting reason, it was not this reason, not the same reason, which was at work in the exposition of the pure state of nature, where, if it was a different reason, it was that of the heart. In fact, one can argue that the state of pure nature is well and truly the exclusive object of the heart, on condition that 'heart' is taken to mean what I have said: reason guided by the principles of the heart. One can argue that the state of pure nature is well and truly the decisive point at which the heart intervenes, in so far as it is the heart which, firstly, posits its concept; secondly, posits its necessary existence; and, thirdly, posits its determinations.

First, the heart posits its concept. This is what distinguishes it from the reason of the natural law theorists, who, for reasons we

---

1   Rousseau, *Discourse on the Origin of Inequality*, p. 24: 'Let us begin by setting aside all the facts, for they have no bearing on this question.'

2   Ibid., pp. 15, 24–5. 'I have . . . ventured a few guesses'; 'hypothetical and conditional reasoning . . . conjectures based solely on the nature of man'.

now know, were incapable of 'digging down to the roots', as
Rousseau says, hence incapable of reaching the concept of the state
of nature in its purity, since they never thought in anything but
impurity, in the false origin. Reason is the impurity of the concept:
this was the circle of denaturation. The heart is the purity of the
concept: this is the solution, at once necessary and impossible, that
is discovered by following a new path. The fact that the heart must
be pure to reach the purity of the concept of the origin will perhaps
involve us in new aporias, but the fact is there: the concept of the
state of pure nature, which is simply the pure concept of the state
of nature, is posited by the heart, or by a reason in which the voice
of the heart speaks. The heart posits its existence as well, and this
positing too is pure. Why? Because the existence of the pure state
of nature is not something observable, and it is not observable
because this state has utterly vanished from the face of the earth,
because nature is lost.

We can find traces of the savage state on earth. For example, we
can observe the savage in the Caribbean, the archetypal savage,
who occurs frequently in Rousseau's work. Thus we can observe
the oldest state of savagery; but, says Rousseau, this oldest state of
savagery is very far removed from the state of pure nature. This
state of savagery is already a form of denaturation. We can also find
children in the woods who have been raised by animals, by wolves;
everyone knows that the eighteenth century was very fond of
discoveries of this kind.[3] But, Rousseau says, these children are just
animals; the proof is that their cries are animal cries. The origin has
thus been lost for ever, and its existence is not observable; yet the
discourse of loss can be pronounced only if its existence is first
posited. To say that the origin has been lost, its existence must be
posited. Observation, however, cannot posit the existence of the
pure state of nature, since that state is not observable, nor can
reason, since it does not possess its concept. Only the heart can.

3   Ibid., Note C, p. 87.

This 'state that no longer exists', says Rousseau, 'and perhaps never did [this phrase was most likely for the theologians] and probably never will, but about which we should nevertheless have accurate notions in order to judge our present state properly'.[4] It may well be asked whether the function of the disappearance of every trace of existence of this state of pure nature is not to isolate it in its purity, shielding it in advance from all possible observation this time so as to reserve it for positing by the heart. And if it has never existed – assuming that this reservation is not meant for the theologians – it is perhaps to preserve it from the danger of ever becoming an object of factual observation, leaving it for the heart in all its purity. This loss would in that case be not an empirical loss, but a de jure loss: since the state of nature can only be lost, can exist only in the form of loss, of present non-existence, its existence could be posited only in the form of a de jure non-observability; it could, that is, be posited only by the heart. We might add that the heart ultimately proves the attributes of the state of pure nature, the contents of this state.

Of course, the man of the state of pure nature has arms and legs like you and me, and the conformation of the man of today. This neutral personage is endowed, however, with precise determinations: independence, solitude, the immediacy of instinct, self-love, freedom, pity, absence of language, absence of reason, and so on. All these determinations are posited as originary, and neither observation nor reason play any role in this positing. It is hard to avoid hypothesizing, therefore, that the positing of the concept, existence, and contents of the state of nature is the heart's specific domain. We will be convinced of this if we make the comparison with Rousseau's subsequent exposition, with everything that follows this positing.

For, in what follows, from the state of savagery on, we have observable facts at our disposal, which, albeit few and far

4 Ibid., p. 15.

between, suffice to mark off the stages of the history of denaturation. It is here that we must, as Rousseau says, observe accurately
and combine observation with reflection. And, together with
factual observation, we now see the intervention of ratiocinative
reason, conjectural reason, and the role of the hypotheses that
contrast with the pure and simple positing of the pure state of
nature. The role of hypothesis and conjecture is to propose likely
explanations in order to connect the observable facts to each
other and fill in the existing gaps in the long process of denaturation. 'I have begun a few lines of reasoning and ventured a few
guesses', says Rousseau, 'less in the hope of answering the question than for the purpose of clarifying it and reducing it to its true
proportions . . .' 'Because the events I am about to describe might
have happened in several ways, I admit my choice between these
possibilities must be conjectural: but besides the fact that those
conjectures become reasons when they are the most probable
ones we can infer from the natures of things, [they] represent the
only means we can have for discovering the truth.'[5] I shall read
you the rest in just a moment.

Conjectures and hypotheses, then, hence the exercise of reason,
but under the dominance of the principles posited in the state of
nature, pure nature; and, secondly, under conditions such that
the conjectures, since they depend on these incontestable first
principles, cannot lead to different conclusions. Here is what
Rousseau says at the end of the text I just quoted: '[T]he conclusions I infer from them will not thus be conjectural, since, on the
basis of the principles I have established [those of the state of pure
nature], another system could not be devised without the same
results and from which I could not draw the same conclusions.'[6]
If this is so, I believe we can defend the following theses.

_____   _____

5   Ibid., pp. 15, 53.
6   Ibid., pp. 53–4.

Recourse to the heart is not just a phrase in Rousseau; the heart is not just a psychological faculty brought to bear, in a modality specific to the heart-faculty, on objects that it shares with other faculties. In Rousseau, the heart is a philosophical power, the power that resolves the antinomies of reason and society, the power of the true origin, separate and pure, pure of all contamination by denaturation or the effect of denaturation: the circular projection of the result onto the origin. The power of the separate origin, and pure, the heart is, properly speaking, the power of the pure concept of origin; that is, the pure or separate positing of this concept; that is, the pure or separate positing of its object and the pure or separate positing of its determinations. This separation and this positing are observable in the second Discourse. We may add that the heart marks itself off from denatured reason in order to posit the pure concept of the origin in its separation. It does not do so, however, in order to flee reason; quite the contrary, it does so in order to save it by transforming it under its dominance, under its guidance, under the guidance of the principles of the heart. Reason is thus everywhere present in the demonstrations of the second Discourse, but it has freedom only under the principles of the state of pure nature and on the condition that state represents.

If, with these results in hand, we now turn back to our starting point, we can observe the following. Of all the philosophers who think in the origin, Rousseau is, we said, the only natural law philosopher to have confronted and upheld the idea of the origin, the idea of the concept of the origin in its structure and applications, and the only one to have subjected it to a radical critique. He conducts this critique, however, as a critique of the false origin alone and in the name of the true origin, in which he thinks and which he posits as concept, existence, and contents. Formally, then, we remain in the origin, and we may legitimately ask: What can the distinction between the false and the true origin really change in all of natural law philosophy? What can the distinction between the state of nature as Locke and Hobbes understood it

and Rousseau's state of pure nature really change in natural law
philosophy? What is the isolation of the state of pure nature?
What, when all is said and done, does the essential difference that
manifests the difference between the natural light of reason and
the natural voice of the heart come down to? What, in the final
analysis, can this difference really change about the basic philosophical commonality embracing all the natural law philosophers
who think in the origin, Rousseau included? Can the variation, in
the form in which we observe it in Rousseau, of an invariant,
namely, the idea of the origin, have the slightest effect on this
invariant's structure? Can this variation, in the form in which we
observe it in Rousseau, have the slightest effect on the nature of
the object that constitutes this invariant's signified?

This is where the plot thickens. We should take note of the
following. For the unique form of the origin that he finds in his
predecessors and contemporaries, Rousseau substitutes two
origins, the false and the true. Thus the origin is redoubled and a
distance is opened up in it, a distance between the false origin,
which is criticized, and the true origin, which is posited. It is the
distance between the error of his contemporaries' circularity –
where the result is thought as its own cause in the origin – and the
true in Rousseau, where the origin is thought as pure, that is, as
separate from its result and utterly different from its result. To the
circle of an originary specularity – which is simply a justification
of accomplished fact and the form par excellence of the philosophy of the accomplished fact, of the philosophy that thinks in the
accomplished fact – Rousseau thus opposes another, pure form
of origin, one not compromised in its result, one so absolutely
separate from its own result that we may even wonder whether it
has a result that we can call *its* result. Rousseau opposes an origin
as a different world, separated from our world by something like a
distance or an *abyss* [*abîme*], an insurmountable distance: an
origin whose purity and separation are reflected, or would be
reflected, precisely, in this abyss.

Rousseau thus opposes and proposes an idea of the origin
that is at the same time, by all necessity, an idea of radical separation, of radical purity – in short, an idea *of the abyss*. I use this
word in order to draw particular philosophical resonances from
it, but it is a word that Rousseau himself repeatedly uses. This
idea that Rousseau proposes is no doubt hard to uphold, but it
is an absolutely necessary idea, an idea that is absolutely necessary if Rousseau wants to think in the origin while also upholding
his radical critique of the origin. If Rousseau wants simultaneously to maintain the imperative of the origin – outside which
nothing about what has occurred, that is, about its loss, can be
understood; nothing about what exists today: society, law,
government, inequality, or human passions in the struggle for
goods, prestige, and power – if Rousseau wants simultaneously
to maintain this imperative and to reject the perpetual speculary
play of the false origin, where the answer never does anything
but precede itself in the form of the question, this poses a serious
problem.

I mean simply this: the redoubling of the question of the origin
has nothing of the redoubling of the shadows cast on the back wall
of Plato's cave by figures moving past in the sunlight. Although
Rousseau's intervention redoubles the origin, the true origin is not
the false origin's double, it is a completely different origin. The
heart is not simply reason's double, it is a completely different
power. As far as the origin is concerned, we may say that the heart
is the power of the completely other. The origin is not redoubled
the way Hegel's *one* divides into *two*. It is the completely other
which divides the origin, and it is the intervention of this
completely other, in other words, of the concept of purity, of the
concept of separation, that is inscribed in the coupling of the true
origin with separation or the abyss – if by this notion of separation
or abyss we understand, simply, the void created by the radical
separation of the pure and the impure, nature and the denatured,
by their absolute non-identity, their void, a void which, if it is

taken seriously, must be thought one way or another, that is to say, must manifest itself in thought.

For, for as long as it is not thought, this void, this purity, this separation that Rousseau requires, demands, calls for – this void remains problematic and we remain uncertain, not knowing whether Rousseau has given us nothing but words, that is, the expression 'pure nature' without a concept, or whether he has committed himself to [s'est engagé dans] the concept of pure nature, the concept of purity, the concept of separation. What is more, we do not know, if these words are indeed concepts, what the meaning comprised by these words, comprised by these concepts, is. To say that we do not know what their meaning may be is to say that we cannot anticipate these concepts' theoretical or philosophical effects on the basis of what has been said so far. For if it is true that a philosophical concept's meaning is its effects, we cannot anticipate these concepts' philosophical or theoretical effects.

For instance, at the point we have now reached, if we ask ourselves the question – What is the meaning of the redoubling of the origin in Rousseau? – we have every reason to suppose that all Rousseau's work on the concept of the origin may concern the concept of the origin alone, that is, a concept supposed to exist in itself somewhere, which Rousseau endeavoured to remodel in a certain way: a remodelling of a form of philosophical thought that would, in some sense, leave its object intact. In the case to hand, what the meaning of the accomplished fact of the essence of society, law, and the state would leave intact is the meaning of the grand categories in which this object's conceptual genesis is thought in natural law philosophy: that is, the meaning of the state of nature, the meaning of the contract, the meaning of the civil state, and so on. For as long as it is not thought in its object, this concept of purity, separation, or the abyss puts us before the accomplished fact of the philosophy of the origin and of its object, and its object of the philosophy of law – that is, law and law alone.

In other words, the question that arises is whether it is merely a matter – to put things in simple terms – whether it is merely a matter, in Rousseau's texts, the second Discourse and *The Social Contract*, of the object that is also in question in Hobbes and Locke. Is it a matter of the essence of government? Is it a matter of the essence of law? Is it a matter of the essence of social relations? Or is it a matter of something else?

I want to suggest that it is a matter of something else and that we can say so because it so happens that Rousseau thought this concept – of purity, separation, or the abyss, if you like – in its object. This idea is registered in Rousseau's works in a certain number of passages of *The Social Contract*, but, above all, throughout the *Discourse on the Origin of Inequality*. The result of this idea of Rousseau's is quite surprising. In other words, I would like to point out that the critique we have been following up to now, which I have explained in somewhat abstract fashion, perhaps, shows us that what is at stake in this redoubling of the notion of the origin is not a certain way of treating Hobbes's and Locke's objects. At stake is the appearance – in profile, perhaps, but the appearance in person nevertheless – of a new object.

That is what I meant to say in suggesting that the result of this thought of Rousseau's – inasmuch as Rousseau did not merely utter words, but tried to think what he was saying – is really quite astonishing. In other words, the difference that goes to work on [*travaille*] the concept of the origin and distinguishes the false origin from the true origin in Rousseau opens up a new space for a new philosophical object. In other words, in this separation that Rousseau carries out before our eyes, which seems to bear only on already existing objects, there appears an object that did not exist before. It is this object that Rousseau proposes to us. We shall see what the meaning of this object is when we move on to the second moment of this lecture, which I announced last time. The first moment, you will recall, was the concept of the origin. The second

point in this lecture could be entitled: 'The moments of the genesis of the second Discourse and their theoretical effects'.

We are going to put the following two propositions, with which
we are familiar by now, side by side. First: withdrawal of the circular origin and, consequently, the necessity of positing an altogether
different, non-circular origin. We shall now write a second proposition, which will serve as the starting point for our exposition: the
necessity, given this first proposition, of positing a genesis altogether different from the classical geneses of natural law philosophy,
an altogether different genesis that sets out from the non-circular
origin required by the first proposition.

In other words, in the genesis that is specifically Rousseau's, we
shall see emerging, as its effect, the difference between the origins.
We shall see what is at issue in the difference between the origins,
what is at stake there, emerging in preliminary form in the specific-
ity of the genesis inscribed in the second Discourse, *On the Origin
of Inequality*. For, in the second Discourse, Rousseau introduces
something that is completely new, if we compare him with his
predecessors. He introduces, if I may be allowed this paradoxical
expression, a new, and quite disconcerting, structure of genesis.

Why disconcerting? Because it is completely different from his
predecessors' genesis. It has been said about the genesis which, in
Hobbes and Locke, brings us from the state of nature to the civil state
by means of the social contract that it is not a real genesis, that it is
not a historical genesis, that it is merely a genesis of essence. I think
this thesis is perfectly defensible and perfectly correct. It has further
been said that Hobbes's and Locke's genesis introduces nothing new,
nothing new other than a philosophical–juridical justification of
the established order or the order to be established. Rousseau saw
this perfectly well in his critique of the false origin. Everything is
already present in the origin: the principles informing the end are
already contained in the origin, as the result is already contained in

the origin. That is why nothing happens in the genesis; it is not a hist-orical genesis. And that is why it is merely a genesis of essence, why the genesis introduces nothing new, why it is linear and continuous.

We can very schematically verify this very general remark, borrowed from Rousseau, by observing that, in the guise of natural law, one and the same essence is at work from first to last in Locke and Hobbes – whether it is fear in Hobbes (we never leave it, from the state of war to the civil state under the sovereign's power) or natural law in Locke (we never leave it, whether it is a question of the state of nature or of its weighted redistribution in the civil state). In Hobbes as well as in Locke, then, the genesis is nothing but a correction, a secondary rectification, or a redistribution of the elements, which are the elements of one and the same essence. We never leave the continuity of essence, and that is why we have to do with an analysis of essence alone. Ultimately, it may be said, the grand thesis of the philosophy of natural law is that one never leaves natural law; one remains in its essence from first to last, inasmuch as the real law and politics that we know are merely reflective modifications of it, the purpose of which is to eliminate the extreme disadvantages of the state of nature.

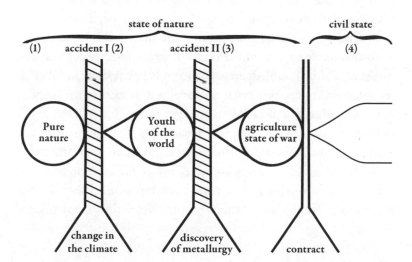

In the second Discourse, Rousseau confronts us with a genesis that is quite surprising, because it is completely different from this genesis of continuity. As a function of, precisely, the critique of the origin and the refusal to project the result onto the origin, Rousseau offers us a genesis whose schema I shall sketch here.

The genesis of natural law separated by the social contract, the genesis of the second Discourse, is constructed this way. It has four moments. The first moment is the state of pure nature, which is to say that it is the pure origin in its separation. Why? Because the state of pure nature would have reproduced itself endlessly if big cosmic accidents had not intervened, that is, the change of the seasons, the cataclysm of the oceans, and so on, which force men to come together. That is, men who were living in the state of dispersion, in the universal forest, the vast forest in which they were lost and separated from each other and in harmony with nature, find themselves forced by that same nature to group together; and, from that moment on, something new begins. There begins the second stage of the state of nature, which comprises three degrees. A first state begins, a first stage, in which, under the impact of external constraints, man's faculties develop at the same time as they are denatured. This is the beginning of a long process that we might call a process of maturation and denaturation, which begins with the beginning of the state of non-pure nature and runs down to the social contract.

In this second phase of the state of nature, men begin to come together and to establish among themselves a certain number of complementary relations that are favoured by need, proximity in space, and mutual assistance: they begin to invent language, begin to invent reason, and so on. This development continues until the moment it reaches a kind of point of satisfaction, of maturation, the point at which it starts going round in circles, exactly as the primitive state of nature had gone round in circles. This is what Rousseau calls the state of the 'youth of the world';[7] it is the state

---

7   Ibid., p. 62.

in which humanity would have preferred to come to a halt, if man had had the choice. This state of the youth of the world is a state in which there reigns what Rousseau calls 'independent commerce' [*commerce indépendant*].[8]

The expression 'independent commerce' has a very precise meaning. 'Commerce' means relations of men with one another. 'Independent' means relations of men with one another in which no man is subordinated to another. Each man's life is independent; that is, a free, mutual relation of men with one another. At this point, things would have gone on indefinitely if a second historical accident of universal scope had not intervened. It was not, this time, the work of external physical nature alone; men no doubt had a part in it, although we do not know how. The result, in any case, was the invention of metallurgy.

The invention of metallurgy is the second big accident. 'Accident' should be taken to mean something which is not precipitated by previous developments, and which changes everything. Metallurgy makes the development of agriculture possible, and, from the moment that agriculture begins to develop, men gradually settle in the forests, or learn how to win ground from the forests. After a certain point, there are no more forests: all the forestland is converted into fields, men's property. And, since the earth is round, men will now find no space in which to settle unless they fight those already occupying it, unless they engage in conflicts with those occupying the first tracts of land won from the forests. We then have the state of war.

The third circle, as you can see, sanctions the third phase of the state of nature. It is after the state of war that men, seeing the trials and tribulations to which they have been exposed, decide to conclude a social contract in order to establish the civil state in the society of men; they do so in the very special forms of the second Discourse, that is, on the initiative of the rich. You can see this

---

8   Ibid., translation modified ('independent activity').

quite extraordinary structure. First, a state of nature broken down into three stages; then a state of pure nature, completely isolated from the rest; then this state of nature, broken down into three phases, with the first two separated by natural accidents, and the second and third separated by another accident that is not simply natural, but is an accident nevertheless. Finally, the social contract intervenes to establish the civil state. Let us say that this structure of the state of genesis is quite surprising, compared with what natural law philosophy has bequeathed to us.

I believe we can say, at first glance, if you will, that what emerges from this schema is that, contrary to what we see in Hobbes or Locke, Rousseau's schema shows us differences that are irreducible, essential modifications, modifications of the essence, discontinuities of essence, and leaps in the process. We may say, broadly speaking, the following: what happens at the end is not reducible to what happens at the start. This genesis is therefore discontinuous. If it is discontinuous, it can no longer be a simple analysis of essence. If it is no longer a simple analysis of essence, it is because it concerns a new object which it produces by its functioning, an object that has to do with something other than mere law, the theory of the essence of law or the essence of the political. It is an object that has to do with something that we must clearly call *history*.

We are going to examine this structure a little more closely. We shall see that, compared to the classic structures, it is literally dismembered. Where continuity held sway, what is imposed are particular forms of discontinuity. The genesis is punctuated by major, profound gaps, breaks, and hiatuses. Let us try to make all that a little more precise.

Firstly, what strikes us right away is that the state of nature is dismembered. Rather than one and the same essence unifying the state of nature, whether it is war and fear in Hobbes, or natural law and peace in Locke, we see the state of nature cut up into three discontinuous moments:

- pure nature;
- the state of nature down to the genesis of the world that we could call the state of peace;
- the state of nature down to the state of war that we could call the state of war.

Between each pair of states of the state of nature there is a discontinuity, the intervention of chance occurrences, hence of causes external to the internal process and bearing no relation to it whatsoever: interventions whose effect is to make it possible to leave the endless circle of repetition or reproduction of the endpoint previously reached. These are thus very special discontinuities, for the external causes, the chance occurrences that intervene between (1) and (2) or between (2) and (3) – these chance occurrences intervene at the very moment at which the process is caught in a circle, that is, reproduces itself on itself, goes round and round as if on a wheel. Thus the intervention of chance, of causes external to the process, presents itself as a contingent but necessary prohibition [*sanction*] of the circularity of a process of reproduction incapable of developing. The state of pure nature is incapable of leaving itself by itself; chance occurrences must intervene. The state of nature of peace, let us say, cannot leave itself by itself; a chance occurrence, the invention of metallurgy, has to intervene. In other words, there is coincidence, second-degree chance, between the intervention of chance and the situation in which chance intervenes. It is as if the situation of endless circularity required chance, because this situation cannot leave itself by itself.

Second remark: these circles – when things turn around themselves by themselves, reproduction that cannot leave itself – which coincide with the intervention of external causes are all, with one exception, results of a process, a genesis. All these circles – the circle of the state of peace, if you will, the youth of the world, the circle of the state of war – are the results of a previous process. But the circle of the state of pure nature, for its part, is not. It is a circle that has no past, that has no genesis, that is the result of nothing, that is its own positing in reproduction, in repetition, that is outside all history. Yet it is that setting out from which a genesis, albeit impossible, will become possible. This genesis, however, will be a discontinuous genesis, and this genesis will be a genesis whose cause is not contained in the state of pure nature. More exactly, it will be a genesis of which the state of pure nature, that is, the state of origin, is not the beginning. In other words, things begin [*ça commence*] after the origin.

What is perhaps still more striking, however, is not just that the state of nature is dismembered, but also that which advenes between the state of war and the civil state, between (3) and (4) – that which advenes at the moment of the contract. You will recall what we said about the civil contract in Hobbes and Locke: the matter is obviously very complicated, but we can nevertheless affirm that, in both of them, the contract, albeit a form that intervenes in order to reorganize a preceding state, is a form that stands in a continuity of essence with the preceding state. The contract intervenes in order to redistribute, to limit, natural law; but it is natural law which limits itself and redistributes itself. It might seem that this is the case in Rousseau too. Not at all. Beneath the seeming identity, we in fact discover a profound difference.

In what does this difference consist? In the fact that the effect of the contract in Rousseau is neither to limit natural law nor to redistribute forces deriving from natural law; the effect that the contract has in Rousseau is the constitution, a constitution, of a radically new reality. In Rousseau, the contract is constituent [*constituant*]. This is what Rousseau expresses by saying that it is necessary to 'denature man', an astonishing expression. Let me remind you that we are at the end of the process of denaturation, the process of denaturation that begins with (2) and ends at the end of (3). Thus we are at the moment of the social contract, the end of the process of denaturation, of the loss of original nature. And the contract must consist in denaturing man. 'Good social institutions', Rousseau says in *Emile*, 'are those best fitted to make a man unnatural [*dénaturer l'homme*], to deprive him of his absolute existence and give him a relative existence... Plato only sought to purge man's heart; Lycurgus has denatured it.'[9] And, in *The Social Contract*, Rousseau declares that 'one who dares to undertake the founding of a people should feel that he is capable of changing human nature, so to speak'.[10]

We could cite countless other passages, but what is important is the word 'denatured'. If we keep it in mind, the arrangement of the schema that I've put on the blackboard will take on an additional meaning. For what happens between (3) and (4), between the state of war and the civil state, is well and truly a discontinuity that is of a very special type compared with other discontinuities; it is not the same kind of discontinuity. Rather, this type of discontinuity, which Rousseau calls a 'denaturation', must be related, if it is to be understood, to another discontinuity, the one between (1) [on the one hand] and (2) and (3) taken together [on the other]; that is, the discontinuity between the state of pure nature and all the rest of the process of the state of nature; that is, what happens in (2) and (3); that is, the process of denaturation.

If this is so, the leap, the constituent discontinuity of the social contract in Rousseau, is intelligible as denaturation only if it is a denaturation of the existing denaturation – in other words, alienation of the existing alienation, in other words, negation of the existing negation. I am using these terms deliberately; you will see why a little later. If, accordingly, this constituent discontinuity

---

9 Jean-Jacques Rousseau, *Emile, or Education*, trans. Barbara Foxley, Indianapolis: The Online Library of Liberty, 2011, p. 11, translation modified.

10 Jean-Jacques Rousseau, 'On the Social Contract', in *On the Social Contract with Geneva Manuscript and Political Economy*, ed. Roger D. Masters, trans. Judith R. Masters, New York: St Martin's Press, 1978, p. 68.

discontinuity stands out against the backdrop of the preceding result, the result of the process of denaturation inaugurated by the leap or discontinuity that brings about the shift from (1) to (2), and also by the discontinuity that brings about the shift from (2) to (3), then we see that what happens in (1), in the state of pure nature, is not just the condition for what happens in (2) and (3) (assuming that we have the two leaps or the two discontinuities that I pointed out to you), but also, beyond (2) and (3), by leaping over (2) and (3), over the whole of this genesis punctuated by the two discontinuities we just saw, that which happens in (1) is the origin of what happens in (4). That is, it is the raison d'être of what happens in the social contract, in which, at the end of the process of denaturation of the denaturation, originary nature finds itself restored, but on new bases. 'To re-establish human nature again on new foundations', as Rousseau says.

If all these remarks are well founded, they obviously entail a number of consequences. I would, however, like to point out to you right away that we have so far remained on a purely formal level; that is, we have observed these discontinuities as inscribed at that level. We have to go beyond these formal descriptions. That is, we have contented ourselves with describing a discontinuous genesis to bring out certain features of this discontinuous structure. We should not, however, forget that, just as the structure of the analysis of essence in Hobbes and Locke concerned philosophical objects and, through them, political objects – we should not forget that what Rousseau is putting into place also concerns objects: first of all, the objects of classical theory, that is, natural right, natural law, the state of nature, the state of war, the social contract, and so on.

What I would simply like to point out here – we will, I hope, soon see it more clearly, in detail – is the following. If the structure of the form of justification and presentation of the essence is changed – you can see the form it takes here in Rousseau – in other words, if the form of genesis is changed, if what had constituted it, that is, its continuous identity, is changed, and if genesis now appears as discontinuous (with specific discontinuities, different in each case), chances are good that the nature of the objects that this genesis is charged with sustaining, is charged with justifying, will find itself, if not turned topsy-turvy, then at least affected. And if we go a bit beyond formal description, we can in fact see that the simple formal dispositive that we have just examined has the following consequence: the classical categories of natural law become problematic and sometimes even unrecognizable.

I shall examine three points. First point: the state of pure nature. To begin with, I would like to justify this term, because I do not believe that it is commonly accepted; I would like to point out several passage in which Rousseau talks, in the second Discourse, about the first state of nature. Let us say that, on at least six or seven occasions, he uses the expression 'state of pure nature' or 'pure state of nature', distinguishing this state from other, later states, and so on. When he talks about the pure state of nature or first state of nature, it is always in order to distinguish it from later states, that is, in order to exhibit it in its separateness: 'how far these peoples already are from the pure state of nature'.[11] The state of nature in its purity, which Rousseau opposes to the state of nature into which the fruit of a state of excessive corruption, the state of despotism, falls,[12] and so on. It is, I believe, easy to provide textual accreditation for the term.

On the basis of this dispositive of genesis, the status of the true origin represented by the state of pure nature becomes problematic and all but unrecognizable; that is, a natural law philosopher can, literally, no longer find his bearings in it.[13] It is necessary to begin

---

11   Rousseau, *Discourse on the Origin of Inequality*, p. 61, translation modified ('from the first state of nature').

12   Ibid., p. 82.

13   TN: The French idiom here translated as 'find his bearings in it' means, literally, 'no longer recognize himself in it'.

with this state of pure nature because it commands the whole critique of the old origin, and because it is its separation which initiates all the rearrangements of the classic, linear dispositive of the genesis. It is, in other words, the fact that this state was isolated at the outset which initiates the whole series of discontinuities and the strange form of the genesis. The state of pure nature, however, has a paradoxical status. Why? Because, firstly, the origin must be an origin; and, secondly, because, as we know, it must not contain the result itself in abstract form. Consequence: the origin must therefore be the non-result, that is, the negation of the result, that is, the radical absence [*néant*] of any result. Thus the state of pure nature will necessarily be, in Rousseau, the concrete figure of the radical absence of society, the radical absence of social relations, the radical absence of sociability, the radical absence of natural right, the radical absence of natural law, and so on. How is it possible to represent radical absence? Rousseau does in fact represent it: he endows it with a concrete figuration that might be called *Gestaltung* in the Hegelian sense. It is the realization of this negation.

Here I shall sketch a few of its general features. Rousseau represents man not as a man (at this point, this is the essential precaution he takes, one of the essential precautions, so as to eschew any projection of the result onto the origin), but as an animal: both less-than-animal, in the sense that man does not have certain faculties that animals do – in particular, crows, who have a language, whereas men in the state of pure nature do not speak – and also more-than-animal, in that man has, for example, an undifferentiated instinct: he can live on any kind of food, which is not true of animals, and so on. A man, then, in the animal state, living in dispersion and solitude – dispersion being one modality of solitude – living in the instantaneousness of the instant, the instant of need, the instant of life, the instant of sexual relations, the instant of death as well (he dies without noticing it, for example, and also lives without noticing it, at the limit) – encountering other men only by accident and in such a way that the encounter never establishes any lasting bond, for the other wanders off into the forest, so that one man never encounters another twice. The encounter is subject to the rule that 'you will never encounter me twice, and every time you encounter me, you will lose sight of me'.

Behind all these concrete figurations, we discover the following: we discover that man, whom no rationality, sociability, need, or language brings close to other men (for nothing of all that exists) – we discover that this man can only live in this state of absolute solitude on one condition: the relationship he maintains with what Rousseau calls nature, which is obviously physical nature, or the relationship physical nature maintains with him. This nature is obviously quite special. It is at once a nature in which there are no seasons, for the weather is always fair: that is, a nature in no way hostile to man, and also a nature that offers him both sustenance, immediately, in easy reach (fruit; all he need do is stretch out his hand), and repose (the shade of a tree, or the refuge of a tree if he is pursued by wild animals, and so on).

This nature is, then, the forest. I believe one can say that the forest in the Rousseau of the second Discourse is a concept, not an object. *The forest is the truth of the state of nature*, the concept of the state of pure nature, the condition for realizing the solitude and the condition for realizing the non-society that define man. It is a nourishing, protective forest, full because it offers men all they need, instantaneously, immediately, without labour; yet it is simultaneously empty – above all empty, because it is a space without places. It is the infinite, empty space of dispersion and the simple encounter with no morrow. The forest is a space without place, a space without *topos*. This space of the forest is at once always present, in the form of nourishment and refuge, and always absent. It is the realization of the existence of the state of pure nature.

The important thing is that recourse to the forest is indispensable for Rousseau if he is concretely to figure this state of pure nature. In the nature of the forest, Rousseau has to look for and find the conditions of possibility for the existence of the state of pure nature. For, plainly, he must conceive of, must think, what the existence of non-social men with no social bond might be. When I told you that Rousseau thought separation, thought purity – here we are at the very heart of this question. What does it mean to think this separation? It means thinking non-sociability, the total absence of bonds among men, utter solitude. On what condition of possibility is this solitude possible? It clearly has to be thought: the concept of this condition of possibility is the forest, is nature, this nature in this form. Thus it is nature alone, that is to say, a certain disposition of nature, the forest plus the permanence of the seasons, or, rather, the absence of seasons, which makes it possible to think the state of pure nature.

However, a crucial consequence appears: the foregrounding of man's relation to nature throughout the dispositive of the genesis, in order, precisely, to meet the requirements of Rousseau's argument. Nature is introduced into the theory from the outset of the pure state of nature (I mean physical nature); it is introduced there as a substitute for society to make it possible to think a humanity in the zero state of society, the state of the radical absence of society. We may say that the forest is the society of non-society. And the nature introduced into Rousseau's thought, into the genesis, by this theoretical requirement, will remain there and play a determining role there to the end.

This is one of the most surprising effects of the redoubling of the origin in Rousseau. Rejection of the circle, rejection of the projection of the result onto the origin – in other words, the refusal to grant any social character at all to the origin – prompt the appeal to physical nature as the solution to the problem of filling this void, of allowing this void to exist. The existence of radical absence [*néant*] is nature, is the forest. The fact that it has, of course, a mythical form in the state of pure nature does not matter much. What matters is that it is introduced into the system, and necessarily introduced there, as a substitute for that which the critique of the false origin has, in all rigour, expelled from it.

The fact remains that this state of pure nature, thought in this way as the radical absence of any social category, must be an origin, must be the good origin. It is a paradoxical situation: if it is an origin, it must be the origin of something, of the result; at the same time, however, it must not contain the least trace of this result. What can be done to resolve this problem? The fact is that Rousseau resolves it, using basically two means . . .[14]

To begin with, Rousseau attributes several different qualities to the man of the state of pure nature: four qualities, three of them positive, and another that is the quality of these qualities. The first three are self-love, freedom, and pity. The last, the quality of these qualities, is perfectibility. What is important in these four qualities is the pair self-love-pity, for this pair represents the virtual nucleus of the natural right of the future, of natural law, and of morality. Invoking the pair self-love-pity, which is a purely animal pair, since Rousseau says it is characteristic of animals as well as men, Rousseau rejects the classic thesis that identifies natural right and natural law with reason. Hence he wants to assign natural right a foundation prior to reason, which results from the development of human history – since reason itself results from the development of human history.

Rousseau accordingly posits the bad origin's very opposite in the origin. That is, he puts the animal movements in it, which he will not discover again at the end, and, in particular, the heart in the form it takes in animal existence, namely pity. I do not subscribe to everything that is said about these subjects in the second Discourse, but it is interesting to see how Rousseau tries to cope with what he here imposes on himself – these two contradictory requirements.

We have to go further.

---

14   TN: There is a gap in the tape recording here.

The essential feature of pity, which is the only relation to exist in the state of nature – compassion for one's fellows – is a purely negative relation; it does not create a bond between men, who, moreover, do not encounter each other. It merely prevents them from harming each other if they should happen to meet. It is, I insist, a negative relation; thus, it is not sociability, social need, need for others – absolutely not; it is simply compassion, it is not harming others, not making a creature of one's own kind suffer. It is therefore purely negative; this is how things would play out if men happened to meet.

I say 'if they happened to meet', for, in the state of nature, they practically never do. That is the most surprising paradox in Rousseau. The originary qualities that he attributes to men in the state of nature have practically no existence, no use, no meaning there. For example, the freedom that he attributes to man, along with the metaphysical qualities, has absolutely no existence in the state of nature; one does not at all see what role it could play there. It is simply there in abeyance [*en attente*], but it serves no purpose. Pity, in its turn, also has practically no existence there – practically none, because men practically never meet, or, at any event, never meet twice. Pity, too, is in abeyance. As for perfectibility, it has no occasion to come into play, since the essential feature of the state of nature in which perfectible men live is that it repeats itself, thus ruling out all progress.

We may therefore say that Rousseau resolves the paradox involved in having to think an origin separate from any result by attributing qualities to man which are, firstly, not social and, in particular, animal; and which are, secondly, theoretically or practically virtual, including the virtuality of these virtualities known as perfectibility – which is expressly said to be of no use in the state of pure nature, although it is attributed to men. In the state of pure nature, men have qualities that are of no use, but are simply there in abeyance, waiting to be reclaimed in the world of the social contract.

That is the first solution. The second solution, however, is much more imposing. It is the one in which Rousseau posits the origin and cuts it off from all genetic continuity of birth with its result: it is the utter powerlessness of the state of pure nature to develop. The origin is trapped in a circle, which I have depicted. It is the perfect adequation of man with nature; nature is good, and so on; men are very well off there; everything goes endlessly round and round, and nothing makes it possible to leave it. The origin cannot leave itself by the logic of its inner essence. The inner essence of the state of pure nature is the inability to develop on its own. The inner essence of the origin is therefore to be incapable of producing any result.

It is in this way that Rousseau does the most to guard against the origin *of the* result, against this little 'of the'. He cuts. No development, no sequel, a state without sequel. At the limit, the origin is the origin of nothing. At the limit, it is posited in the form of negation as such. Here is what Rousseau says: 'After showing that perfectibility, the social virtues, and other faculties that natural man received as potentialities could never have developed on their own, that to do so they needed the fortuitous convergence of several external causes that might never have arisen and without which man would forever have remained in his primitive condition', and so on.[15]

I now come to the sequel. We who read Rousseau and discuss him know that this origin, which is an 'origin of nothing', is nonetheless the origin of present-day human society; we know, that is, that a result has taken place. It is the confrontation between this origin – of which the conditions of existence constitute the negation – and the result of this origin which is powerless to produce anything that will confer its meaning on the powerlessness of the origin and this having-taken-place, this result that has taken place. It therefore seems to me that the powerlessness of the origin is a

---

15   Ibid., p. 53.

rejection of linear genesis, that is, a rejection of the analysis of essence; but, for this reason, it is, in the structure of the origin, the inscription, in its radical separation from any result, the inscription of another idea: the idea of separation, that is to say (now we have made a little progress!), the idea of events foreign to the essence of the originary state, the idea of the *having-taken-place*: 'to do so they needed the fortuitous convergence of several external causes that might never have arisen and without which man would forever have remained in his primitive condition'. The idea, in other words, not just of events, but of the contingency of events; in other words, the idea of advening, of taking place, and the idea, as well, of the necessity produced by these events. In short, a thought that inevitably revolves around – revolves around, and inevitably tends towards – something like history.

It is not, however, the state of pure nature alone, about which I have just said a word or two, that becomes problematic in Rousseau. All the master categories of natural law philosophy do too. Natural right and natural law, for example: it takes the whole material genesis of the state of nature to constitute them. They only begin to become effective at the end of state (2) and the beginning of state (3), before being engulfed by the state of war. To make their constitution possible, the external conditions allowing the virtual principle (which I mentioned earlier) of natural right to take form must be fulfilled; in other words, the conditions that allow pity to become morality.

Why external conditions? Why the intervention of these chance events? Because the internal conditions of the state of pure nature are powerless to bring about their development; because external nature in the form of the big cosmic accidents must force men to come together and become other in order to meet their needs and, accordingly, transform or begin to develop the first gestures of sociability among themselves.

Once the state of pure nature is posited as separate, thus lacking an internal logic of self-movement or self-development, the

pre-social principles of natural right can develop only under the
impact of external conditions. 'Taking form' – that pity should
take form, and take the form of morality – 'taking form' means
something very precise in Rousseau. It means inscription in forms
produced and prescribed by external constraints. That is why these
notional realities, such as natural right, natural law, or sociability,
must appear problematic. The same holds for sociability, reason,
language, and, as well, the state of war – so many problematic
states or faculties.

What can 'problematic' mean here? Two things. Firstly,
Rousseau calls into question the fact that these notions were taken
for granted by natural law philosophy. Rousseau calls into question the fact that these notions were given in the self-evidence of
presence for natural law philosophy, denouncing it in his denunciation of the circle of the origin. These notions are thus problematic
in that first sense: they are called into question, they constitute
problems. They are, however, problematic in another sense as well,
one far more important for us. They are problematic because they
pose a question completely different from the question of essence,
the one that held our attention in this first remark. They pose a
question that is the question of existence. Once the continuity of
essence is interrupted, once the analysis of essence is abandoned,
what becomes a question is existence itself, the conditions of existence of such-and-such a form of the essence.

What is problematic [*la problématicité*] is, therefore, the posing
of the question of existence, of the forms of the advent, the forms of
the taking-place, the forms of the irruption of existence. From this
point on, the genesis becomes a real genesis, occurring in real time
(even if the time that Rousseau is talking about is mythical): real
phenomena that are materially distinct, materially distinguishable.
At this point, new concepts appear in Rousseau's discourse:
concepts such as the concept of accident, the concept of contingency, the concept of event, the concept of the accumulation of
causes, the concept of existence, and concepts in which we can think

other concepts of Rousseau's, such as constitution, irruption, and so on. However, throughout this process of questioning, of problematization, we see the determinant role of the physical nature that intervenes in the genesis. As in the case of the pure state of nature, physical nature has the role of creating the conditions of existence and apparition of the various forms that the origin is powerless to produce. This seems to me to be fundamental in Rousseau.

We can say, then, that the whole dialectic of human development is conditioned by the dialectic of men's relationship to nature. Indeed, after the stable, nourishing, protective nature of the beginning, we see a catastrophic, chequered nature appear with the first big accidents, a nature hostile to men that produces three combined effects on them which will make it possible for them to begin to live together.

First effect: nature forces them to come together physically; it forces them to establish physical contact by assembling them. For example, Rousseau thinks that societies first emerged on islands after big catastrophes . . .[16]

Secondly, nature forces men to develop their qualities in order to satisfy their needs, inasmuch as the course of the seasons has changed and nature is no longer as generous as it was. Men have to work.

Thirdly, nature forces them to help each other in order to satisfy their needs.

It is from this gap between nature and men, this separation between nature and men – whereas, in the state of pure nature, there was no separation between nature and men – that there emerge, conjointly, the first forms of observation, reason, language, social exchanges, the passions, and so on. After a great deal of time has gone by, we observe a transformation of the nature of space; in

---

16   'Great floods or earthquakes surrounded inhabited regions with seas or precipices; upheavals on the globe caused portions of the continent to break off into islands.' Ibid., p. 59. TN: There is a gap in the tape recording here.

certain clearings, huts appear – men go to work building huts. This is extremely important, because it is the introduction, the apparition, of *topos* in interior space, of place. Men now have a fixed place; place appears in this undifferentiated space, the place of huts. This is the moment corresponding to independent commerce and the youth of the world.

The same relationship to nature accompanies all the subsequent genesis from the third moment of the state of nature down to the state of war, after the discovery of metallurgy. The discovery of metallurgy makes possible agriculture and its development. The appropriation of land follows agriculture and changes everything, over two periods. In the first period, says Rousseau, there is still some forest left. That is, men have not appropriated everything; anyone wishing to settle down can settle in the forest. At this time, servitude does not reign among men.

In the second and final period, there is no forest left; it is in this moment that the state of war reigns, because, to appropriate land, proprietors have to eliminate other proprietors; because every man wants to protect himself against attack; because the state of war à la Hobbes, that is, a universal and preventive state, now reigns among men. In all this, however, the relationship to nature is extremely close, as you can see. I therefore think we can conclude that problematizing the notions of natural law philosophy entails, in Rousseau, among other things, the need to bring men's relationship to nature into play as determinant, even if it is mythical, and, very precisely (since he describes it in these terms), the way men obtain their subsistence: the mode of production of men's subsistence.

One more consequence remains to be drawn from the dispositive of the genesis based on the separate origin, the origin as separated, and the origin's powerlessness to develop by itself. If the origin cannot develop by itself, it is because it is pure and separate. If it can develop only as an effect of external causes that disrupt its conditions of existence, and therefore its forms of existence, the inevitable conclusion is that this development can only be contradictory: it will indeed be the development of primitive man's faculties, but under conditions that will denature them. Here we must be clear about what we mean: denaturation, in Rousseau, is not moral denaturation, a transition from goodness to evil, for example, from one quality to another, from one attribute to another, from one opposite to another. To be able to oppose one contrary to another, one has to be in a common element: one has to be, for example, in social life, to which goodness and evil belong. Denaturation, therefore, cannot be the transition from one opposite to another in the same element, because the development of the origin is, precisely, transition to another element. This is an important point. The transition to another element, that of men forced to live in close proximity, subject to need, and so on. Denaturation, then, is necessarily bound up with transition to another element, in which there exist the previous forms that are transported into it.

In itself, this other element – the various forms in which men come together, their enforced sociability as a function of their relationship to nature – is neither good nor bad. The forced precipitation of the originary element and man's originary qualities into the other elements of the state of nature produces antagonistic effects of denaturation. The originary qualities can develop only on condition that they are deformed by this development. They are deformed by the element in which they develop. Gradually, they become unrecognizable, until they reach, at the end of the state of war, the state that is as sharply opposed as possible to the state of pure nature.

Here too, we have to do with a process that is completely different from the process of the genesis of essence as found in Hobbes or Locke, since we have to do with a process of real difference, a process of antagonistic development that takes the form of a process of denaturation or alienation. This denaturation is the separation of the origin from itself; it is the non-identity of identity; it is the developed contradiction of the origin as the other of its result in the result, as the other of the origin.

To conclude these reading notes on Rousseau, I would like to tell you how, as I see it, these ideas, which bear on or turn on history, present themselves in Rousseau. This is directly related to everything I have just told you. In the guise of a theory of natural law, and in the guise of a theory of the true origin, and thanks to the critical redoubling of the origin that we have witnessed, we see the emergence in Rousseau – I do not say that he does this deliberately; it happens, it takes place this way – we see the emergence in Rousseau of an idea that is quite foreign to natural law philosophy, that is not intended by that philosophy, that is not the intentional idea of a philosophy of natural law, and that may even be quite unintentional in Rousseau: the emergence of what I call an idea of history or ideas for a history, for the purpose of elaborating, going to work on, the concept of history, ideas for fashioning the concept of history. What I would like to point out in concluding is that, if we examine the matter at all closely, we do not have to do with a single body of ideas with which to elaborate the concept of history; we have to do with a double corpus, in other words, with a double idea for history, with a double idea about history.

We can range this duality of thought under a division that would, first, put what happens in the state of pure nature in relation with what happens in the civil state. In other words, let us put the state of pure nature and the state of the social contract in relation; that is, we put the origin and the end in Rousseau in relation, what must plainly be called the origin and the end, whatever the calamities that separate this origin from its end. We have, after all, reached the end and are in it; there is nothing to be done about it; and even if all that was contingency, that is just how it is now. We are in the end, and it is here that the social contract intervenes, which is the denaturation of man and the denaturation of the denaturation.

At this point, the process appears to be, from beginning to end, an antagonistic process, since it is a process of denaturation; at the same time, it is a teleological process, since the end is the origin restored. That is why we can say that Rousseau is the first theorist to have thought history in the category of the negation of the negation, the first to have thought the historical process as a process of antagonistic development in which nature is negated, the negation is negated, and originary nature is re-established on new foundations.

The theorist who expounded this thesis is Engels: you will find two pages in Engels in which he defends this thesis – I don't have the time to read them to you – in *Anti-Dühring*. I'll read you the end of the passage nevertheless:

> Already in Rousseau, therefore, we find not only a line of thought which corresponds exactly to the one developed in Marx's *Capital*, but also, in details, a whole series of the same dialectical turns of speech as Marx used: processes which in their nature are antagonistic, contain a contradiction; transformation of one extreme into its opposite; and, finally, as the kernel of the whole thing, the negation of the negation.[17]

The negation of the negation is the whole of the *Discourse on the Origin of Inequality*.

I think that this thesis can be put to polemical use, and I realize that it can perhaps be defended with respect to Rousseau. The comparison with Marx seems more suspect to me. As far as Rousseau is concerned, I would simply say this: this theory of alienation – if we were to take it seriously, simply by saying: nature at the origin, denaturation of the denaturation, hence restoration of nature in a new element – neglects, in Rousseau himself (I am talking about Rousseau alone, I am not talking about what one

---

17   Friedrich Engels, *Anti-Dühring (Herr Eugen Dühring's Revolution in Science)*, in *Marx and Engels Collected Works*, vol. 25, London: Lawrence and Wishart, 2010, pp. 129–30.

might say about him), a crucial theme, the theme of the conditions
of existence of this process. We know that these conditions of
existence are thought in Rousseau, broadly speaking, by means
of the concept of physical nature and of man's relations to nature.
In other words, the radical interiority presupposed by the process
of the negation of the negation or denaturation of the denaturation is contested in Rousseau himself by the following idea: that
one must posit an exteriority in order to think the process of interiority. An idea of exteriority is required to make the process of
pure interiority possible.

I shall not say anything more about this form of interpretation,
this form of an idea for history. I would like to point to another
idea that is present in Rousseau and that seems to me more
important, more original. It too, perhaps, is an idea that no one
has noticed, as I told you last time.

For my part, I would single out the following themes.

First, if we examine this whole genesis in Rousseau, we observe
that there are beginnings without origin that take three forms in
Rousseau. First, the accidents. We have said enough about them
for you to see how the thing intervenes: absence of an internal
dialectic of development, external accidents intervene and things
take off, whereas, previously, they were on a treadmill. Second
form of beginning without origin: the irruptions that come about
in very odd phenomena that are circles, circles once again – but
not the ones we have discussed so far. These circles are mentioned
by Rousseau in connection with the problem of the origin of
languages, the origin of reason, and the origin of inventions. Each
time, in connection with these three very precise examples, which
Rousseau examines, he elaborates an antimony and explains that
the result is required to produce the result; that is, that knowledge
of languages is required to establish languages, since men have to
enter into an agreement to be able to agree on words – thus they

have to talk to be able to talk. The same goes for reason, the same goes for inventions. The argument about inventions is a little subtler and more interesting. Rousseau says that men can invent something by chance or discover something by chance; however, as the state of society, the social fabric, is not sufficiently close-knit, sufficiently dense, such an invention would be forgotten almost as soon as it was invented, quite simply because it would not succeed in inserting itself into a system of practices that would preserve and develop it. Consequently, the inventions that society requires in order to develop require society in order to exist.

We have to do with a whole series of circles of this kind. Every time that Rousseau has to do with such circles – which are not at all the same circle as the one we have discussed in connection with the origin – he brings a solution to bear that can hardly be thought otherwise than in the form of an irruption. In other words, he does not know how, but things come to a stop, that is, the circle is broken and something happens which has a purchase on the event that ends up conferring existence – that is, the phenomenon ends up coming into existence, ends up attaining an existence that lasts. That is what I would call, if you like, irruption [*surgissement*]. In the majority of cases in which Rousseau presents phenomena that have a circular form of that kind – that is, *it would have been necessary*, and the like – we always have to do with an index of irruption.

The third type of phenomenon in Rousseau is what can be called 'the creative nature of time'. '[N]o attentive reader can fail to be impressed by the formidable distance that separates these two states. He will see in this slow succession of things the solution to an infinity of moral and political problems that philosophers cannot unravel. He will understand that . . . the human race of one era is not the human race of another.'[18] The slow succession of

18   Rousseau, *Discourse on the Origin of Inequality*, p. 83.

things, the infinite slowness of the centuries, the infinity of time is, for Rousseau, the solution to all sorts of problems he cannot resolve in any other way. In other words, time is endowed with a productive capacity, that is, it is capable of resolving the problems of circles in particular, and it is capable of serving as a substitute for accidents. In other words, from accidents to the productivity of time, you see a whole series of graduations that make it possible to think what we might call the event or the beginning of something.

The second category that seems important to me – it is not thought in these terms in Rousseau, but the thought is there – is the process by which every contingency of historical import is transformed into a necessity. We may say that this is the essence of history, or, rather, that what is historical is necessary and that what is necessary is contingency [*du contingent*] that has been trans-formed into necessity [*en nécessaire*]. This is true of all the accidents that we have observed; it is also true of all the irruptions in the circles; it is also true of the contract. Every time that an important historical element intervenes, there appears what we may call a new historical element, a new element in history. In other words, there is a transition between the different levels; we move from one level to another. Contingency is transformed into necessity, but the necessity created by a new contingency is not the same as the old one. There are differences in degree and level between the necessities.

The third important point seems to me to be the antagonistic development at the heart of necessity, on the condition I mentioned a moment ago, namely, that necessity is brought into relation with external conditions that are absolutely determinant. I would here add something related to what I just said: we may say that, for Rousseau, each phase of historical development sketched in the second Discourse has its own law of development, a law different from the other laws of development.

This position directly recalls an article by a Russian critic quoted by Marx in the second preface to *Capital*, a passage in which the critic says that Marx was the first thinker to maintain that each historical period is subject to a different law.[19]

The fourth point – here we enter extremely ticklish zones – is that, for Rousseau, not every development is self-resolving. In other words, there exist insoluble problems; there are circles (since there are always circles in Rousseau), but there are also circles without a solution. There are insoluble problems: we could say, paraphrasing a famous sentence, that humanity sometimes sets itself problems that it is unable to solve. That is very much in Rousseau's spirit. If we try to put it in a somewhat more conceptual way, we may say that, for Rousseau, there exist external conditions for the resolution of contradictions; that is why there are contradictions without a solution. These external conditions for the solution of contradictions are essentially men's relationship to nature.

Finally, last theme, if you will. It is – since we are talking about contradictions and solutions – the contract. The fact is that there exists a particular solution to this last contradiction, the contradiction of the alienation of the state of war. This solution is that of men's intervention; it is that of the contract, which establishes a new element (once again, we change elements here, hence laws as well, since each element has its own law) – which establishes an element that is new not just with respect to the immediately preceding state, but even with respect to the state of origin.

This solution is interesting; I told you that it is a solution in which the contract is constituent [*constituant*], that is to say, that it establishes (it is not at all a contract – if we analyse it in detail, we realize that the legal form in fact simply masks a veritable mutation) a veritable change of regime, a veritable constitution. We could characterize this solution as one that establishes, in the form of the reprise, a new beginning of the origin.

---

19   Karl Marx, 'Afterword to the Second German Edition', *Capital Volume One*, *Marx and Engels Collected Works*, vol. 35, London: Lawrence and Wishart, 2010, pp. 18–19.

It would be a question, this time, of a new necessity that hinges on human will. What is interesting, but obviously very hard to conceptualize, is Rousseau's acute awareness of the extraordinarily precarious character of the social contract. It is, literally, a leap into the void, as we could show in a study or by citing certain passages. It is something which is not without affinities with the events that proceed from contingency, a certain contingency, events which occurred earlier, but take on another form here, since it is a question of a *human* contingency, that is, of a voluntary act on men's part which involves a tremendous risk. A leap into the void, if you like, so much so that we can say that the whole edifice of the social contract is suspended over an abyss. (I am using this word deliberately, because it is in connection with the contract that Rousseau uses it.) It is in connection with the problem of the social contract that Rousseau says that there exist two abysses in philosophy: the problem of the union of the soul and the body, and the problem of the social contract.[20] When we read the *Contract* and a series of other texts at the same time, we realize that Rousseau did not just have in mind that it could be a question of a theoretical abyss, but also a question of an extremely risky political enterprise.

I shall leave it at that for this lecture on Rousseau.

---

20   'Just as the action of the soul on the body with respect to man's constitution is unfathomable in philosophy [*est l'abîme de la philosophie*], so the action of the general will on the public force with respect to the constitution of the State is unfathomable in politics [*est l'abîme de la politique*].' Rousseau, 'On the Social Contract or Essay about the Form of the Republic' (First version, usually called the Geneva Manuscript), in *On the Social Contract with Geneva Manuscript*, p. 168.

LECTURE THREE

17 March 1972

I SHALL GIVE YOU ONE final lecture today, and stop after this lecture. In this final lecture, I would like to talk to you about Rousseau once again and about the second Discourse once again. I would like to do something somewhat detailed on Part I of the second Discourse.

Last time, we saw the theoretical effects produced in Rousseau by the completely unprecedented dispositive of his genesis, a discontinuous genesis. We saw that these theoretical effects concern a certain number of possible concepts, ideas, and notions that are not made explicit, that are not thematized and, a fortiori, not systematized by Rousseau: hence possible concepts in the free state, in a state of theoretical divagation. We saw that these concepts – they can be so described – designate something which, vis-à-vis the old object of natural law theory, is very plainly a new object: it is what can be called the 'object history', with, of course, all the scare quotes one likes.

We saw, you will recall, the theoretical premises thanks to which this unprecedented dispositive of the genesis was literally imposed on Rousseau. It was imposed on him thanks to his radical critique of the false origin as circular and, correlatively, thanks to the fact that the true origin was posited as separate from the false origin, as pure, since this true origin is the pure state of nature. The simple critical redoubling of the origin, its division, thus had two effects, one triggering the other: first, the discontinuous dispositive of the genesis, of the process of denaturation and socialization; and, second, what I am calling the possible concepts implied by the provocation of the novelty of this dispositive.

However, these concepts, which I would group around the object history – these concepts are merely practised by Rousseau, rather than thought by him. To take just one example: the concept of accident observable between the state of pure nature and the state of peace, or between the state of peace and the state of war – in other words, the cosmic accidents, to begin with, followed by the accidental discovery of metallurgy, which Rousseau calls 'this fatal [*funeste*] accident'.[1] Rousseau practices the concept of accident, inasmuch as he writes the word 'accident', but he does not think the concept that he practices; he brings it into play, but does not reflect on it, on its theoretical meaning. He does not bring it into relation with his other concepts. That is what reflecting a concept would mean.

The consequence is that the concepts that we have brought out around the object history are visible for us, as a result of the analysis we have brought to bear on the structure of the dispositive and of the process of socialization/denaturation, and as a result of our comparative analysis of this dispositive, which we opposed to the classical dispositive of natural law philosophy – and only on that condition. It is only because we have analysed the implications of the dispositive of this process that these concepts are visible for us, but these effects are not visible in the same way [*au même titre*] for Rousseau in his text. It is not that these concepts or effects are invisible in and of themselves; it is not that they do not figure in Rousseau's text, for they do figure in the logic of his text. Rousseau, however, fails to see them, and fails to see them for a simple reason: he directs his gaze

---

1   Rousseau, *Discourse on the Origin of Inequality*, p. 62.

elsewhere. We may say that these effects escape him, in both senses of the word: objectively, because he produces them without explicitly wanting to; and subjectively, because he does not pay enough attention to their existence to reflect it theoretically.[2]

The fact is that Rousseau trains his attention on completely different concepts, which he has forged to make his system function. Indeed, we can say that the concepts that make Rousseau's system function are one thing, and the concepts that the system necessarily produces thanks to its very special sort of theoretical distraction (which we analysed last time) are quite another. Put differently, in order to bring out what is unprecedented in Rousseau, we have so far analysed, above all, the principle of the redoubling of the origin and the effect of that redoubling, the discontinuous structure of the process, and the effects of this effect, namely, the concepts induced by this structure.

We must, however, go on to see how Rousseau makes his system function with his explicit concepts. Since I cannot, in this final lecture, analyse the whole of the process depicted in the second Discourse, I shall take one precise example, the example of the first moment, the example of the pure state of nature, and ask the following question: How does Rousseau manage to produce a representation of this state? What determinations does he attach to it? What is their inner logic? What is the logic of this discourse, and what is the discourse of this logic? I am going to follow Rousseau's text very closely in certain passages; however, to follow it closely, one does well to observe it from a certain distance. I shall therefore remind you that the state of pure nature has to meet – after all that we know, all that has been said about the origin – two requirements.

The first requirement is that the state of pure nature has to escape from the circle of the result projected onto the origin; that

---

2   TN: The 'objective' sense of the word *échapper* (escape) is 'to slip out', as in 'the words slipped out before he could think'.

is, from the circle of the social result projected onto the pre-social, the non-social, from the circle of society projected onto the state of nature. For this reason, the state of pure nature must be a radical absence [*néant*] of society. It must be the absolute degree zero of society. Thus it must be separated, in the strong sense, from everything involving society, from every existing social result. In other words, between society and this radical absence of society, which will be a state, a nil [*néant*] state, of society, there must be a radical separation: not a de facto separation – this is the important point – but a de jure separation, such that the state of nature contains in itself, de jure, this separation itself. The first requirement is that separation not be imposed on it from outside, but result from its inner essence. It is not all that easy to meet this requirement in the representation of a real state.

The second requirement might be stated as follows. The state of nature must be the true origin, must, that is, be an origin in a mode altogether different from that of the false origin; hence it must be an origin in a mode external to the circle. The state of pure nature as origin must therefore contain, in a form to be defined, non-social determinations corresponding to the radical absence of society, determinations which, albeit radically separate in the sense just mentioned, are nevertheless originary, are the origin without being the cause of the contradictory process of socialization and denaturation; and are also the origin, while being, this time, the cause of the denaturation of the denaturation, of the negation of the negation, in short, of the restoration of the state of nature on new foundations at the moment of the social contract. There we have the two requirements.

We shall now see, in detail, how these two requirements are staged [*mises en scène*] by Rousseau; in other words, how the origin *is realized*, a term that must be understood in the strong sense. That is, we shall see how Rousseau confers reality, or something that has the appearance of being a reality, or the signification of being a reality, on the origin, in a concrete theoretical figure, in something anticipating what Hegel will call a *Gestaltung*, that is, a concrete figuration. I say 'in a concrete theoretical figure'. Why theoretical? Because these are concepts that are realized in what Rousseau narrates; that is, concepts embodied in the dispositive of a figure. Why a concrete figure or figuration or *mise en scène*? Why concrete? Because the existence of the concepts has to take on the form of empirical existence so that the origin is truly an origin, existence of the essence; so that space, trees, springs, animals, human individuals, hunger, sleep, death, and so on wind their way through the text. Why a figuration or figure? Because the natural empirical elements figuring concepts have to maintain relations among themselves such that they can ensure the efficacity, hence the theoretical effects, of the system of concepts. Why figures? In order to figure a theoretical system, a system of concepts that command one another.

I believe that this is how we have to read the text of Rousseau's second Discourse. We have to read it not as a naive history, like the stories reported by travellers who have seen savages somewhere in the world and recount the lives of men dispersed in the big forest, with the dispersion of this story's details; rather, we have to read it as a systematic conceptual figure in which the dispersion that is narrated, and its details, are simply the ultimate effect of the system.

This is how I would like to try to read this text. To begin, I shall set out from Rousseau's general thesis, expounded in the state of pure nature. In the state of pure nature, men are free and equal. I take that as my starting point in order to ask the question of the forms of existence of these two concepts. The answer is as follows: men are free and equal in the state of nature on two conditions, to which the division of my study into two parts corresponds. First condition: men are free and equal in the state of nature on the following condition: that man's relationship to nature is immediate, that is, without distance or negativity. Second condition: that man's relationship to man is nil in the state of nature.

Two parts, then. Part I of this exposition: man's relationship to nature is one of immediate, constant adequation.

Rousseau's general thesis may be put this way: between natural man and the physical nature in which he lives, there exists immediate, constant harmony, an instantaneous harmony excluding all distance and all negativity, a constant adequation excluding all variation. His thesis is obviously opposed to the grand classical thesis that depicts man, deprived of everything, confronting a hostile nature. You remember the myth of Protagoras, which has it that Prometheus saw that man was naked and exposed to the cold, whereas the animals were covered with fur.[3] Well, Rousseau's man is naked too, and the animals in the world around him are also covered with fur, yet Rousseau's man does not shiver and is not cold; he is not cold because it is not cold outside. We shall see why it is not cold outside later, but we may say that, for man, nature takes the place of fur.

It is only in the next part of the second Discourse, after the big cosmic accidents that will bring the state of pure nature out of its endless circle, when seasons appear, when trees start to grow – it is then that nature becomes distant and hostile, and that man has to 'wrest' (the word is Rousseau's)[4] his subsistence from it at the price of hardships and labour. At this point, man, in his relation to nature, enters into distance and, through distance, into negativity, into mediations, and thence into language, reason, civilization, and progress. In the state of pure nature, however, man exists in direct proximity to nature, in non-distance, in adequation. If we admit, as a definition of freedom, a thesis of the kind Hegel defends – 'to be free is to be at home', *bei sich* – we may say that this definition accords rather well with the state of pure nature described by Rousseau. Man in nature is at home like a fish in water, we shall say, like an animal in its natural habitat, in its

---

3   Plato, *Protagoras*, trans. W.K.C. Guthrie, in Edith Hamilton and Huntington Cairns, eds, *The Collected Dialogues of Plato, including the Letters*, Princeton: Princeton University Press, 1969, 321c, p. 319. 'Prometheus . . . found the other animals well off for everything, but man naked, unshod, unbedded, and unarmed.'

4   Rousseau, *Discourse on the Origin of Inequality*, p. 55.

element, at home. Man, who is nature, is in nature, is naturally at home, and is therefore free.

The whole opening section of the second Discourse tends to confer a concrete figuration on this thesis, as we shall see in the detail of the text as we discover the successive characteristics of man as animal, of man's body, and of man's needs. 'I shall suppose [man]', says Rousseau, 'to have been at all times formed as I see him today', stripped, however, of 'the supernatural endowments he may have received and all the artificial faculties that he was able to acquire only through a long process [*progrès*]'.[5] This man, shorn of, stripped of, the results of the progress of history, is no longer anything but animality. Man is, therefore, an animal, but an animal of a special sort. He is the generic animal, rather than a determinate animal; for what distinguishes him from a particular animal is that he is the animal 'the most advantageously constituted of all'.[6] We shall soon see how this constitution that is the most advantageous of all is defined.

What does 'being an animal' mean for Rousseau? To be an animal is to be a machine that renovates itself by itself, thanks to the information it receives from the external world through its sensory organs. To be an animal is to ensure the life of one's machine by satisfying its needs; to be an animal is therefore to have needs, and an animal's needs are physical needs. This term is crucial, for an entire segment of Rousseau's thought is based on the distinction between physical and moral needs. Physical needs are simple needs: hunger, thirst, the need for sleep or a female: such are the sole needs that Rousseau grants to animals. They are called simple because they can be satisfied immediately; we shall see why in a moment. Man so defined, as an animal, a subject of simple needs that can be satisfied immediately, is distinct from the animal as such in that the animal has specific instincts, whereas man may well, says Rousseau, have none at all.

---

5   Ibid., p. 26.
6   Ibid.

This makes man an animal of a very special kind, an animal that is not an animal, but what might be called the realization of animality in general, when its particular determinations are left out of account. Each species has only its characteristic instinct, Rousseau says, and 'man, who perhaps has none peculiar to himself, arrogates them all'.[7] Thus man is not defined as an animal by a specific instinct and by specific objects corresponding to this specific instinct, but by the absence of instinct, which is not a pure void, but, on the contrary, a positive capacity to appropriate all the instincts of all the animals.

What is the significance of this specific difference? We may say right away that man is no longer limited to a single instinct, as is every animal species; that is, man is not limited to a single object to satisfy his needs. With all the instincts at his disposal, man is all the more independent of nature. For example, an animal is so constituted that its instinct leads it to look for a particular kind of shelter; man can make do with shelters of all kinds. An animal's instinct leads it to look for certain kinds of food; man can make do with food of all kinds. As Rousseau puts it, man therefore 'finds his sustenance more easily than do any of the rest' of the animals.[8] The multiplication of instincts in man thus multiplies the answers to man's needs in nature and augments man's adequation to nature; in the same measure, it diminishes the negative character of the nature confronting man. Once man appropriates the universality of the animals' instincts, he appropriates the universality of their objects and will at all times find in nature what he needs to satisfy his own instincts.

So much, then, for man's general nature, which is animality.

Let us now see how this becomes more precise when we consider man's body, the first form of naturalness and animality. What characterizes man's body in the state of pure nature is its

---

7   Ibid., p. 27.
8   Ibid.

physical independence, the fact that it needs no external help, no physical help from outside. The whole man is in his body. There is no distance between man and nature, there is no distance between man's body and nature, with the result that man possesses a body that needs no supplement or tools, but directly satisfies itself. 'A savage's body is the only tool he knows',[9] Rousseau says; his tools are its members. All the stronger by necessity, since it does not have tools as modern man does, man's body consequently develops all the more in that it alone provides for his needs. Natural man has the advantage of 'always carrying, so to speak, [his] whole self with [him]';[10] and nature reinforces this form of physical independence. Natural man as Rousseau depicts him for us is strong, and all the stronger in that he must do without any supplement. He therefore concentrates all his strength in his body; his faculties are multiplied, his vision is more acute than civilized man's, as are his hearing, his sense of smell, and so on. In contrast, his sense of taste and his sense of touch are much coarser. You know all these passages; I shall not labour the point.

Man's relation to the body, which, as we see here, implies direct contact with nature, is manifested in another form as well, in the form of illness and death. However, the presence of illness and death does not come between man and his body, as it does in social life. Rousseau gives us two reasons for this. First, illnesses, in a conception modelled after the one Plato develops in *The Republic*[11] – illnesses appear as social institutions, as so many results of the evolution of society. Rousseau complacently develops this thesis. 'The history of human ailments could be written by tracing that of civilized societies.'[12] In the state of pure nature, consequently, since society does not exist, since refined foods do not

---

9   Ibid.

10   Ibid., p. 28.

11   Plato, *The Republic*, trans. Paul Shorey, in *The Collected Dialogues of Plato*, Book 3, 405a ff., pp. 649ff.

12   Rousseau, *Discourse on the Origin of Inequality*, p. 30.

exist, since fatigue, griefs, alcoholic beverages, and the passions do not exist, the man of the state of nature is never sick. Savages know no ailments other than injury and old age. Their 'surgeon' is 'time', their 'regimen' is natural life.[13] They know neither gout nor rheumatism and are consequently spared all illness.

As for death, it is not an evil for man in the state of nature. Why? Here we have another very interesting point: because death is an event that goes unnoticed, because it is a natural event that nature takes pains to hide. Rousseau here develops a Lucretian conception of death:[14] death does not exist, death has no natural being, because no one can perceive it, neither the dead man, who dies without knowing it, without knowing what death is and without fearing it, nor his neighbours, because he does not have any; death thus has no witnesses, neither the one who dies nor the one or the ones who might otherwise see him die. Old people, says Rousseau, 'expire in the end without anyone noticing that they have ceased to exist and almost without noticing it themselves'.[15] This absence of death is the effect of an absence of consciousness; it is the absence of expectation, the absence of any representation of the future, the absence of fear. Animals will never know what it is to die, and since man is an animal, he does not know what it is to die, for this knowledge of death and fear of death suppose an anticipation, the sense of the future that men no more have in this period than animals do.

Thus man is not dependent on the nature of his own body as if it were an obstacle, whether in the form of sickness or death, nor is he subject to the nature of his body as if it were something alien

13 Ibid.
14 Lucretius, *On the Nature of the Universe*, ed. Don and Peta Folwer, trans. Ronald Melville, Oxford: Clarendon Press, 1997, Book 3, ll. 838–45, p. 93: 'So, when the end shall come/ . . . And we shall be no more, nothing can harm us/ Or make us feel, since nothing remains/ . . . And if it were true that mind and spirit can still/ Have feeling torn from the body, that means to us / Nothing.'
15 Rousseau, *Discourse on the Origin of Inequality*, p. 29.

to him. Hence his body is not an obstacle, but the means of his independence, the body of his independence and freedom. Freedom is the body in harmony with itself in an existence in which man's body is in harmony with nature. That is what we shall go on to see now, with respect to needs – for the body feels needs.

Here we observe the same immediacy, the same independence; no obstacles, no distance. Thus we see that needs are satisfied immediately, because they are immediate needs, physical needs. I told you that Rousseau draws an essential distinction between physical or immediate needs and moral or social needs, which are mediated needs; the latter take the detour of an idea or a man, that is, of a representation or an external mediation, and end up multiplying needs and creating artificial needs. Immediate needs, in contrast, are animal needs; they are natural impulses, needs for natural things, physical needs. Man in the state of nature has no desire other than his own physical needs: 'his desires do not go beyond his physical needs'.[16]

The relationship of need to nature, to its satisfaction, is therefore realized without any intermediary, without the detour of ideas, without the detour of a need for men, without the detours of tools. Need is the pure movement of the body turning towards an object of satisfaction found in nature. 'The only goods in the world he knows', says Rousseau, 'are food, a female, and repose.'[17] Nature answers this immediate need, which does not take the detour of an idea, the imagination, or a passion, immediately, through abundance. 'His modest needs', says Rousseau, 'are easily within reach.'[18] This concept is crucial: the object of need is to hand. Hegel, describing paradise, picked up on this concept with the notion of *Handgreiflichkeit*, the 'ready to hand'. Man has only to stretch out his hand, says Rousseau, and his needs are satisfied.

16 Ibid., p. 34.
17 Ibid.
18 Ibid., p. 35.

He also says: 'The products of the earth furnished all the necessary support and prompted him to make use of them by instinct.'[19] He also says: 'The condition of nascent man . . . was the life of an animal initially limited to pure sensations, scarcely profiting from the gifts supplied him by nature, much less imagining he could wrest anything from it.'[20] Man does not have to wrest anything from nature; he need only stretch out his hand, and his needs are satisfied. Thus his needs are modest, but immediately satisfied. His instincts are multiple, since man does not have a specific instinct, so that he can find an object to satisfy his needs at all times. Trees are abundant and, it seems, short, since they will begin to grow when the state of nature ends, making it hard to pick fruit because their branches are so high. Nature is thus in easy reach, immediately; it is not an obstacle standing in the way of needs, but the immediate answer to them; and it is an answer that asks nothing in return: that is, men do not have to work.

It will be objected: But are there no wild animals in this idyllic nature? Rousseau considers the hypothesis. And it will be objected: Are they not an obstacle? Rousseau responds with three arguments.

Firstly, man lives on fruit; he therefore does not have to hunt wild animals in order to eat them.

Secondly, man quickly learns to avoid them; he is more resourceful than they are, and need only climb trees to avoid them. Thus man does not have to face off with wild animals in the event that they attack him.

Third argument – this is a series of interlinked arguments – wild animals do not attack man, because they mean him no harm and he means them no harm. Between men and animals, who are all sentient creatures, there exists a commonality of nature, which is the compassion of sensitivity, the compassion of pity. Animals are sensitive to men, men are sensitive to animals; everybody spares

---

19   Ibid., p. 55.
20   Ibid.

everybody, reciprocally. Pity appears here, for the first time, as the abolition of animals' difference from men.

This harmony between man and external nature, about which I have just told you a little something, appears in Rousseau's text; it is here that we see things becoming systematic, as the condition of the harmony between man and his own body. It is because man is in harmony with nature that he is in harmony with his own body. It is because nature invites him to engage in natural exercise that his body develops. It is because nature responds to his immediate needs with healthy, abundant food that the human body is not sick. It is because nature is not a problem for man that man does not need the mediations of thought, imagination, reflection, and so on, that he does not think about death, that he does not think about his own death, and that he therefore has no problems of life or death with his body.

This immediate harmony is a harmony without distance; it is the harmony of instinct satisfied by nature. [On the one hand,] no difficulties, no problems, no distance, no negativity; hence, on the other hand, no need for reflection. Since nature is the tacit answer to the problems of nature, everything in the state of pure nature is resolved this way, at a pre-reflexive level, thanks to the pure movement of nature prior to all reflection. This phrase of Rousseau's – 'the pure movement of nature, prior to all reflection'[21] – is uttered about pity, but it holds for all the determinations distinguishing the man of the state of nature. Man does not need to reflect, he is in a pre-reflexive state; man does not need to anticipate, for the future does not exist for him; time does not exist for him; and, since his needs are satisfied at once, immediately, man has, Rousseau says, 'no idea of the future', no curiosity, no philosophy.[22]

The amusing example he gives is that of the Carib, who is not a man of the state of pure nature, but a man of the subsequent state

---

21   Ibid., p. 46.
22   Ibid., p. 35.

of nature, whom he cites with even better reason – who, he says, when he has slept in a bed for a night, sells it in the morning, with no thought for the fact that he will need a bed to sleep in that evening. Thus he lives outside any notion of time.[23] And, since the world 'sleep' has been mentioned: if man is a creature without explicit consciousness, if man is a creature who does not know time and who lives in the ongoing repetition of immediacy, his truth in the state of pure nature is, ultimately, sleep. Man, says Rousseau, loves to sleep. 'The savage must love to sleep, but he must sleep lightly, like animals, which think little and may be said to sleep whenever they are not thinking.'[24] Thus, under these conditions, if we suppose that man never thinks, he must sleep a good deal. Here again, we cannot help but recall that, a little later, Hegel will, in the *Philosophy of Subjective Spirit*, elaborate an entire argument about sleep as the harmony of nature with itself.[25] This is prefigured in Rousseau.

Such, then, is natural man's relationship to external nature. Man is an animal who, as such, feels only simple physical needs and can satisfy his needs with fruit that is in easy reach. The adequation between man and nature therefore supposes, first, in man, the form of existence known as animality, that is, simple physical needs; second, in nature, a form of existence such that it is everywhere and at all times in easy reach. You can see that a certain number of determinations have been posited; but they necessarily call for others.

It is here that we first encounter *the concept of the forest* as a form of existence of nature necessitated by Rousseau's theoretical requirements in order to satisfy – a form of existence, a way nature

23   Ibid.
24   Ibid., p. 32.
25   G.W.F. Hegel, *Philosophy of Mind, being Part III of the Encyclopedia of the Philosophical Sciences, together with the Zusätze*, trans. William Wallace and A.V. Miller, Oxford: Clarendon, 1971, section 1, para. 398, p. 66.

has to be made – in order to satisfy, everywhere and at the same time, man's two basic physical needs, hunger and sleep. It is trees which, in Rousseau's text, provide, precisely, fruit and shade for sleeping or as a refuge. Here, however, we must attend to the logic of the system, which imposes a whole train of consequences on Rousseau. So that nature can thus fulfil the conditions for human freedom everywhere, the forest must cover the whole globe: there has to be a forest as far as the eye can see or, let us say, as far as the concept can reach. Still better: the forest must not just be everywhere, but must be the same at all times. This makes it necessary that nature remain constant so that adequation remains constant.

This requires, then, that there be no seasons and that there be no more difference in natural time than in human time; that there be no difference in natural time, this difference being *the* seasons (nature without seasons, in other words, is a nature without time). It requires that nature no more have time than man has time, that the absence of time in the one case correspond to the absence of seasons in the other. It requires that there be, in both cases, repetition of the same, immediate continuity of the same; that there be, in nature, no more distance within nature itself than there is distance within man, between man and his body, or than there is distance between man and his body, on the one hand, and man and external nature on the other.

Thus we have a forest as far as the eye can see and a forest without seasons. Rousseau, accordingly, makes the earth's axis coincide with the ecliptic again in order to abolish seasons, since he explains that it was when the Lord tilted the earth's axis that seasons appeared.[26] In the same way, Rousseau shortens the trees to put fruit in easy reach of all hands, in order to produce the nature that the existence and state of pure nature call for.

---

26   Jean-Jacques Rousseau, 'Essay on the Origin of Languages', in *The Discourses and Other Early Political Writings*, 2 vols, ed. and trans. Victor Gourevitch, Cambridge: Cambridge University Press, 1997, vol. 1, pp. 272–3.

So much for the first condition, the relationship between man and nature.

I now turn to the second condition, the second moment in this exposition: men's relations to each other.

I have already told you that, for the state of nature to realize its concept, men's relations to each other had to be nil. For Rousseau, it is a question of realizing, in the proper sense of the word now, the null state [*l'état néant*] of society in the state of pure nature. It is a question of producing the concrete figure of the non-relation of men among themselves. How can a non-relation be endowed with existence? How can a non-relation, a nothingness, be concretely figured? Such is the problem that Rousseau confronts and resolves. He resolves it by means of a whole series of conditions that he will expound in the result, and the characterization of men as solitary and dispersed: solitary by essence and condition, and dispersed so that nothing can come along to break this solitude.

What is the foundation for this solitude and this dispersion? How does Rousseau found all that, and, at the same time, realize all that? The operation is divided [*se dédouble*] into two moments; this act of foundation is divided into a negative condition that is de jure – this is important – and a positive de facto condition. Everything with a bearing on law will be negative, and everything with a bearing on facts will be positive.

I begin with the negative de jure condition. The negative de jure condition consists in the rejection of the theory of man's natural sociability. This theory of natural sociability is, as you know, one of the major theoretical stakes of the philosophical-political polemics for which natural law provides the stage. The important thing is that we witness a historical reversal between the sixteenth and eighteenth centuries. At a certain moment, in the beginning, between the sixteenth and the eighteenth century, it can be said that one's attitude towards the social contract and the theory of natural sociability constituted the touchstone for the philosophical-political positions adopted in a certain domain. That is, broadly speaking, the avant-garde, those in the opposition, the anti-feudal theorists, were at once for the social contract and against natural sociability. Hobbes, for example, is opposed to the theory of natural sociability. In contrast, natural sociability is invoked in this period, as a rule, by philosophers who defend the feudal order and refer to Aristotle. And, for the feudal party, the theory of natural sociability is always the correlate of a theory of men's natural inequality.

In the eighteenth century, however, we see a spectacular reversal with regard to the theory of natural sociability. We see a revival of this theory based on bourgeois, not feudal positions, as may be observed, for example, in Pufendorf, Physiocrats such as Mercier de la Rivière, the *Encyclopaedia* (I refer you to Diderot's article 'Society'), and so on. We find, consequently, a slightly different presentation, which remains substantially the same, but is inserted into a theoretical apparatus that confers a completely opposed political meaning on it.

To provide some idea of the prehistory and continuity of the theory of natural sociability, we have to say, very, very briefly, a word about the way it presents itself in Aristotle. We find this sentence in Aristotle's *Politics*: 'Man is by nature an animal made for civil society.'[27] Even if people did not need one another – need in the physical, material, utilitarian sense – they would still feel the desire to live together. In truth, common interest assembles us as well, but civil society is less a society of life in common than a society of honour and virtue. Natural sociability in Aristotle is thus divided [*se dédouble*] into two forms of sociability: utilitarian sociability and virtuous sociability.

We find the same thesis and, broadly, the same distinction, but drawn with much greater precision and force, in the eighteenth

---

27 Aristotle, *Politics*, Book 1, chap. 2, 1253a. Althusser probably used the translation by Marcel Prélot (*Politique*, Paris: Gonthier, 1964, p. 62). Aristotle's sentence is more commonly translated 'man is by nature a political animal'.

century, in the Encyclopaedists and, after Pufendorf, in the Physiocrats. The idea that man is naturally sociable because he needs society, that man is made for society, becomes, in the eighteenth century, the idea that man is naturally sociable because he needs society in two senses. First, man needs society materially, as a means of satisfying his own needs, which he would be incapable of satisfying by himself. This is, accordingly, a utilitarian need, material and utilitarian. What is more, second, man needs society to satisfy his need for man, that is, for friendship and for society in the moral sense of the word. Here, for example, is what Pufendorf says: 'The social attitude is cultivated by men in order that by the mutual exchange among many of assistance and property[28] [this is, then, utilitarian], we may be enabled to take care of our own concerns to greater advantage.' He adds: 'Nature has ordained a certain general friendship between all men, of which no one is to be deprived.'[29] Thus we have the twofold theory of man's material need and moral need. Man needs man materially and morally.

We find a blanket rejection of this twofold theory in Rousseau. For him, man does not naturally need man; that is, man is not at all affected by such a spontaneous need deriving from his nature, grounded in his nature. Man naturally needs neither the material assistance of men, hence society, to satisfy his needs, nor men's moral society, friendship, or companionship. In the *Discourse on the Origin of Inequality*, Rousseau repeatedly returns to this theme: nature has done little to prepare men's sociability. Rousseau renounces natural sociability as a foundation for natural law. He founds this natural law on pity and self-love, 'with no need here to

---

28   TN: Althusser's translation reads *commerce de secours et de service,* 'exchange . . . of assistance and services'.

29   Samuel Pufendorf, *De jure naturae et gentium*, ed. Walter Simons, Oxford: Clarendon, Classics of International Law 17, 1934 [1672], vol. 2: *On the Law of Nature and Nations*, trans. C.H. Oldfather and W.A. Oldfather, Book 2, chap. 3, para. 18, pp. 213–4. The French translation that Althusser cites may be found in Robert Derathé, *Jean-Jacques Rousseau et la science politique de son temps*, Paris: Vrin, 1970, p. 143.

introduce the principle of sociability'.[30] Thus he openly declares his opposition to the thesis of natural sociability.

These positions are obviously of the very first importance. For it was essential, for Rousseau, setting out from the premises we saw last time, to avoid conceding anything at all to the thesis of natural sociability in either of its forms – man needs man because he loves him and, equally, man needs man because he is useful to him – lest he lapse into that for which he criticized his contemporaries and predecessors: the circle of the bad origin, the circle of the result projected onto the origin. By attributing sociability to men, for whatever reason, one brings society straight into the state of pure nature, which must remain a state of non-society. That is why Rousseau must at all costs reject the two foundations of society, material need and moral need.

He acquits himself of the task with great consistency (we are here in law [*droit*], though it is a question, precisely, of doing away with all law) in two famous theories. [First,] the theory which has it that physical needs, taken by themselves, far from uniting men and bringing them together, disperse them – an astonishing, paradoxical theory, one that makes sense only as a counter to, and refutation of, the utilitarian theory of the Encyclopaedists (that is, of the whole eighteenth century), which has it that men's natural needs, their material needs, bring them together. Rousseau says: 'It is claimed that men invented speech in order to express their needs; this seems to me an untenable opinion. The natural effect of the first needs was to separate men and not to bring them together . . . the necessity to seek their subsistence forces [them] to flee one another.' These passages are drawn from the 'Essay on the Origin of Languages'.[31] There we have the first thesis: men's physical needs disperse rather than assembling them.

---

30 Rousseau, *Discourse on the Origin of Inequality*, p. 17.
31 Rousseau, 'Essay on the Origin of Languages', *The Discourses and Other Early Political Writings*, vol. 1, p. 253.

The second theory in which Rousseau acquits himself of this task is the theory which has it that the only relation among men in the state of pure nature is not that of a need for man (sympathy, human love, and the like), but the negative relation of compassion, the negative relation of pity, which is a relation existing among all sentient creatures, men and animals. Rousseau thus rids himself of this danger by clearing the decks with this twofold negative theory, which ensures that man has no need at all for man, whether material or moral.

But that is not all. It is not all, and Rousseau does not believe that he has settled the score with the theory of sociability once he has rejected its theory of man's material need and man's moral need (sympathy, friendship, love, and so on). Rousseau in the second Discourse, and this is quite unexpected, also criticizes at considerable length something that plays, in him, the role of a theory of what might be called perverse sociability, the role of destructive sociability, which he descries in Hobbes as the theory of man's wickedness. Thus Rousseau describes natural man as 'wandering in the forests, without work, without speech, without a dwelling, without war, and without ties, with no need of his fellow men and no desire to harm them'.[32] The desire to do harm that appears in this short quote, a desire that is placed side by side with war, that figures after war, is here situated at the same level as man's need for his fellow men.

For it is possible, at the limit – and this is what Rousseau does – to present the desire to do harm, if it is natural in man, as a form of bond that would unite man with man in competition, violence, and war. If one grants that man is naturally inclined to harm man, one grants that man needs man in order to be a wolf to man – to be not his friend, but his savage beast; one grants that man needs man as the object of his wickedness. And one could make this aggressive instinct a form of sociability, the perverse form of sociability, an

---

32   Rousseau, *Discourse on the Origin of Inequality*, p. 51.

unsocial sociability that would impel men to live in society solely in
order to tear each other to pieces and do each other harm.

Such is the thesis that Rousseau pretends to ascribe to Hobbes,
taking pains to refute it at the same level as the other two theses
about sociability. He refutes it, of course, by repeating his major
argument against Hobbes: that he projects onto the origin of society passions which develop only with society itself, and imagines
that war might be waged from man to man on the basis of a perverse instinct present in every individual, whereas war presupposes
constant relations. Rousseau generalizes: what is said about wickedness could and should be said about goodness too, for virtues as
well as vices, to be worthy of their name, presuppose established
relations among men: the material relations of social constraints
reinforced by intellectual relations and relations of passion.

At the limit, therefore, man in the state of nature can no more
love man than he can hate him, can no more desire man's welfare
than he can wish him harm. In the state of nature, man can no
more be called good than wicked, since the state of pure nature is
prior to all relation between men, is separate from, and foreign to,
any relation; it does not so much as contain the germ of a relation
in any form of sociability whatever, right side out or inside out,
positive or perverse. 'In the state of nature', says Rousseau, since
men 'have no kind of moral relationships to each other', and no
common 'duties', they can 'be neither good nor evil'.[33] 'savages are
not wicked precisely because they do not know what it is to be
good.'[34] Rousseau concludes his critique of Hobbes by saying:
'There is, moreover, another principle that Hobbes failed to see . . .
the one natural virtue . . . I speak of pity.'[35] With that, we have
come to pity, that enigmatic concept that necessarily surges up
to counterbalance the three forms of the theory of sociability.

33 Ibid., p. 43.
34 Ibid., p. 45.
35 Ibid.

So much for the de jure conditions, which are negative. That is, Rousseau rejects every form of sociability in man.

We must now turn to the de facto conditions, which will be positive. For man's solitude is not founded on a negative de jure condition alone; it is also founded on a positive de facto condition.

For once sociability and need have been declared unthinkable in the following terms – 'it is unimaginable why, in [the] primitive state, one man would need a fellow man any more than a monkey or a wolf needs its fellow creature'[36] – the following riddle remains to be explained. Granted, men do not naturally feel any friendly or hostile inclination towards each other, no inclination leading them to unite. Granted, as well, that men do not naturally feel a need to turn to other men to satisfy their physical needs. It remains to explain why they are not forced to do so and why they can dispense with this. This point is crucial, since we know, from the subsequent process of socialization, that men gradually began to become sociable because they were forced to come together by harsh natural conditions, and that, once brought together by nature's inclemency, they began to associate in brief encounters, followed by more enduring associations, in order to satisfy their needs. Thus it remains to explain why men, who do not have the slightest natural need for society, are not forced into society in the state of pure nature; why they can remain dispersed and, consequently, can remain solitary.

They can do so because there is no distance between their physical needs, which constitute all their needs, and the object that satisfies them. Men are not forced into society, that is, into coming together, because nature is always present and immediately close, and is always and at all times the ever-ready answer to the demands of need. It is this immediate proximity between man and nature, between need and its object, which makes it possible to understand why needs disperse men. Men's dispersion is the obverse [*l'envers*]

---

36   Ibid., pp. 42–3.

of nature's proximity. Men are distant from one another because nature is close to each of them, anywhere and everywhere.

The limit situation in which this paradox and this effect of reversal appear is the imaginary one – for it practically never occurs in the state of nature – in which two men find themselves disposed by some chance event to seize the same piece of fruit in order to meet their needs, and to quarrel over it. From this situation – the origin, you will recall, of the state of war in Hobbes – Rousseau simply draws the following conclusion: the men would have no reason to enter into competition; on the contrary, each would have every reason to go look for his fruit on a different tree.[37] Far from coming together to help each other or tear each other to pieces, the men would go their separate ways of their own accord, both in order to satisfy their needs and because such satisfaction is possible everywhere.

But while men may well part from each other, they never part from nature, which is always equally close to them. Ultimately, that is why their physical needs can part them. Men part because they avoid each other, and they avoid each other because they have nothing to gain from coming together; they can avoid each other because nature never parts from them. Nature is their real society.

Setting out from this twofold condition, in which fact reinforces right, in which the positive de facto conditions reinforce the negative de jure conditions, Rousseau turns his efforts to the details of his panorama, until he has eliminated every possible trace that might suggest the possibility of interhuman relations. This is the work of a theoretical craftsman; it is not as easy to accomplish as all that . . .[38]

———

37 'Does a dispute sometimes arise over a meal? He will never come to blows about this without his first comparing the difficulty of winning with that of finding his sustenance elsewhere.' Ibid., Note I, pp. 95–6.

38 TN: There is a gap in the tape recording here.

For man does not need man; yet he doubtless does need woman. The physical need for females is one of man's animal needs. How does Rousseau extricate himself from this dilemma, how does he get out of this predicament? He gets out of it by means of a series of very long considerations which effectively prove that it is not easy to get out of it.

He gets out of it, first, by means of a distinction between the physical and the moral in love; that is, by means of a distinction comparable to the one which led us to distinguish moral need from the physical need we discussed a moment ago – that is, he simplifies the form of sexual need to an extreme. He makes it an animal need, without representation, without imagination, without consciousness of the future, even, at the limit, without self-consciousness, and without a capacity for identification – that is, without recognition of one's partner.

Rousseau gets out of it, second, by attributing morality in its entirety – that is, sentiments, ideas, relations, and ties – to society, while attributing the physical alone to the state of nature. Yet that does not change the fact that man needs woman. Rousseau gets out of it, third, thanks to the physical anonymity of natural man's love. Any woman is good for natural man, Rousseau says, speaking of the sexual encounter; he speaks, however, of man, and does not say that any man will do for any woman (this point of view could not yet be made reciprocal in this period). '[F]or him, any woman is good.'[39] This is crucial, because, at the limit, an individual woman does not exist in the sexual encounter. In the sexual encounter, one's partner is unidentifiable. In other words, after the encounter with one's partner, one no longer knows who one's partner was. In other words, man no longer knows who he went to bed with.

Finally, Rousseau gets out of it by means of the thesis – a fundamental thesis, because it is directly opposed to the thesis which Locke defended at length – that woman has, between conception

39   Ibid., p. 49.

and childbirth, no reason to bind herself to the man she has encountered. As you may recall, Locke made it a duty of natural law for a man to remain by a woman's side between conception and childbirth and during the children's upbringing, until such time as the children were capable of leaving the family home.[40] All that was based on natural law and was inscribed in Locke's nature.

Rousseau explains that a woman has no reason to bind herself to the man she has encountered, and that a man has no reason to bind himself to the woman he has encountered, because, in any case, they do not know what has happened, for one thing and, for another, are incapable of recognizing each other. Neither knows who the other is and they cannot find each other again. Moreover, since they roam through the forest, they lose sight of each other as soon as the first tree comes along.

All this is coherent – could, at a pinch, be coherent in an imaginary world. The only real problem is that represented by the children, since it must be admitted that the woman nurses them, so that they remain with their mother for a certain time, leaving as soon as they can. This is a real problem, which Rousseau will draw on, which he will turn to account later, when he says that it is likely that the invention of languages was due to children. Languages are invented by children, the first rudiments of language are invented by children, and then they are able to talk to their mothers.[41]

On this whole question, I refer you to Note L of the second Discourse; you will see how adamant Rousseau is.[42] Whether his

40   John Locke, 'The Second Treatise of Government: An Essay Concerning the True Original, Extent, and End of Civil Government', in *Two Treatises of Government*, ed. Peter Laslett, 2nd edition, Cambridge: Cambridge University Press, chap. 7, para. 79, p. 337: 'For the end of *conjunction between Male and Female*, being not barely Procreation, but the continuation of the Species, this conjunction betwixt Male and Female ought to last, even after Procreation, so long as is necessary to the nourishment and support of the young Ones, who are to be sustained by those that got them until they are able to shift and provide for themselves.'

41   Rousseau, *Discourse on the Origin of Inequality*, p. 38, and Rousseau, *Emile*, p. 32.

42   Rousseau, *Discourse on the Origin of Inequality*, Note L, pp. 110–13.

theses are more or less convincing is another matter; at any rate, he engages in an extraordinarily sustained theoretical effort to reduce anything in sexuality that might resemble the beginnings of a human relationship to zero, or to nearly nothing. To reduce this relationship to nearly nothing is to reduce it to a very precise concept in Rousseau, the concept of the pure, fortuitous encounter.

It will be granted, on the strength of Rousseau's premises, that the encounter in sexuality is fortuitous inasmuch as men who are dispersed can encounter each other only by chance. Sexual life, however, is a physical need that brings individuals together. This meeting, however fortuitous, must therefore be without duration. That is how Rousseau gets out of trouble. It will be granted that the sexual encounter is without duration if the instant of the encounter coincides with the instant of the sexual act, which is purely animal, that is, takes place between partners who have no means of representation, imagination, or identification at their disposal that might enable them to recognize their partner or anticipate subsequent events.

This category of the *encounter*, which we have just seen emerging in connection with sexuality – the encounter as chance event without duration or sequel, as instantaneous chance event – is the category in which Rousseau thinks, in general, everything that can transpire between men in the pure state of nature. Men live dispersed, they live in solitude, but it sometimes happens that they encounter each other by chance, and it is by chance by definition, it is by definition that it does not last, it is by definition that it never has consequences, that it has no sequel. For men never meet twice and, if by chance that should happen, it would be the first time for them, since, unable to make comparisons, they are unable to identify themselves; unable to identify themselves, they are unable to recognize each other; unable to recognize each other, they are unable to remember each other, and so on. At the limit, 'the first time' itself means nothing at all.

Obviously, there are very many passages on the encounter in the second Discourse. '[W]ithout fixed dwellings or any need for each other, they might meet up scarcely twice in their lives, without recognizing or speaking to each other.'[43] '[N]early the only way to meet up again was to keep each other in sight.'[44] '[F]inding almost certain refuge in the trees, [man] may take on or leave any encounter, and make the choice between flight or combat', and so on.[45] There are very many such passages.

To come, now, to the most interesting passage: if a man were ever to find himself in a position to take another man captive, Rousseau explains in a passage that I am going to read to you, and to want to reduce him to slavery, in short, to bind the man to himself by means of fear, the slave would only have to wait for his master to fall asleep at the foot of a tree, and he would be free; he would flee into the forest, where he would never be seen or captured again, since, by definition, the forest is where men never see each other twice:

> If someone chases me away from one tree, I am at liberty to go to another one; if someone harasses me in one place, who will stop me from going elsewhere? [My master] would have to resolve not to let me out of his sight for an instant . . . [S]uppose his vigilance momentarily slackens? Suppose an unexpected noise makes him turn his head? I slip twenty paces into the forest, my chains are broken, and he never sees me again in his life.[46]

We may conclude from this that, on condition that the sexual encounter is reduced to the minimum, Rousseau thinks, in the form of the encounter between men in the infinite space of the forest

---

43 Ibid., p. 37.
44 Ibid., p. 38.
45 Ibid., p. 28.
46 Ibid., pp. 52–3.

through which they roam, the absence of all bonds between men. The encounter is the punctual event that has the property of effacing itself, leaving no trace behind, surging up out of nothingness to return to nothingness, with neither origin nor result. Later, after the state of nature has been surpassed, the forced, enduring encounter obviously takes on a completely different meaning in Rousseau, but, from the theoretical standpoint, it is quite symptomatic that there figures, in the state of nature, an encounter in the zero state, just as there figures a society in the nil state, and that Rousseau assigns these two concepts the same condition of existence: the infinite space of the forest, a space without place.

There we have, then, with a few details, all the determinations that Rousseau is obliged to deduce as so many a priori conditions in order to answer the question of the state of pure nature. This question is: What must man be, what must nature be, and what must man's relationship to nature be for men to have no relations among themselves, for the state of pure nature to be a state of the radical absence of society?

Here are the essential features of the answer: man must, first of all, be an animal who realizes the concept of generic animality, in that he has only physical needs that can be immediately satisfied. That is the first condition. The second: nature must stand in immediate proximity to man, must at every step offer him 'storehouses and shelter',[47] as Rousseau puts it, in easy reach, always more abundant than his needs, everywhere and at all times.

This is where the deduction of the forest begins, since the tree is the synthesis of storehouse and shelter, shade and refuge – as well as the deduction of the universal forest, so that man can find something to eat everywhere in it. The deduction of the forest, however, goes beyond this omnipresence, this omni-generosity. It is more than the immediate answer to physical need; it is the space of men's dispersion, an infinite space, a space such that it prevents all

47   Ibid., p. 27.

encounters from producing the least tie. The forest is the space of non-recognition, of non-identification, of non-identity.

Positively, therefore, the forest is defined as the immediate object of man's physical need; negatively, it is defined as the form of space that allows men to avoid being forced into society. It is a space without place in which men are subject to divagation, in which they do not run the risk of binding themselves to other men because they cannot bind themselves to space. The universality of the fullness of the object and of the void of the encounter and place: that is what the forest is. Because the forest realizes this double requirement, it is, in the strong sense, the concept of the conditions of existence of the animal man in the state of pure nature. When it ceases to be in conformity with its concept, when trees grow taller, when seasons appear, man will no longer be at home in nature. He will be obliged to wrest his subsistence from it; places will appear in the space of the forest; men will be forced to come together; and the process of socialization will begin.

A condition of existence of the state of pure nature, the forest is also the concept of its endless repetition, its repetition without difference. The forest is repetition, always the same, in all places and at all times, space without the difference of places, time without the difference of seasons; it is the counterpart of the instantaneous repetition – without the difference of memory, without the difference of signs and ideas – of physical need in man. This speculary face-to-face between man and the forest, man and nature, is itself an immediate repetition of adequation without difference. It is this twofold immediate repetition, commanded by [sous] the immediate repetition of its adequation, which allows the system to function. It is this face-to-face and the double repetition which allows the system to function in Rousseau, but on one absolute condition: pure repetition. Thus the state of pure nature is the state of the simple reproduction of its conditions of existence.

Nothing happens in it. It merely repeats itself; it contains no productive [*efficace*] difference, no principle of development, no
driving contradiction. It cannot leave itself; it lasts indefinitely.

That is what Rousseau says in the second Discourse. 'After
showing that perfectibility, the social virtues, and other faculties
that natural man received as potentialities could never have developed on their own, that to do so they needed the fortuitous
convergence of several external causes.'[48] '[T]he generations multiplied unproductively, and because each began anew from the same
point, centuries passed by in all the crudeness of the earliest ages,
the species was already old, and man remained ever a child.'[49]

This powerlessness to leave itself here appears, in Rousseau's
text, as a *consequence* of the determinations of the concrete figure.
In fact, it is the principle governing them. What Rousseau here
deduces is, in the form of powerlessness to leave itself, the concept
of the true origin's separation; he simply rediscovers what he
'deduces' here, because it is the very concept that it was a question
of realizing – the separation of the true origin from the false
origin, hence the origin as separate.

Thus we see the origin as separate now, as realized in this Rousseauesque figure. The question that arises is the following: If the
origin is radically separate, in what sense can it still be called an
origin, and of what can it be said to be the origin? Do we not have
to do, rather, with a beginning – a beginning, moreover, with
no sequel?

Precisely because this beginning with no sequel has had a
sequel, it is not a beginning, but an origin. And this beginning
with no sequel was only able to have a sequel because the sequel
was not *its* sequel; this beginning with no sequel thus contained
something enabling it to have a sequel [*de quoi avoir une suite*]
that was not its sequel. That is why Rousseau can consider it to be

48   Ibid., p. 53.
49   Ibid., p. 51.

an origin – because of this 'something enabling it to have a sequel'.

The fact that its sequel is not its own is revealed rather clearly by the endless circle in which the state of pure nature goes round and round. Only accidents can break this circle and initiate a forced development. This forced development must, however, be a possible development; in other words, natural man must have a nature and be capable of modifying his nature in response to the pressure and constraint of circumstances. This nature is known: it is animality. This capability has a name: it is what Rousseau calls perfectibility, a faculty peculiar to man which, virtually, dissociates him from the immediacy of generic animal instinct and endows him with the power to change and acquire new dispositions and new faculties: intelligence, reason, ingenuity, arms, but also the social passions, and so on.

What is originary in the state of origin would thus be something like perfectibility. If, however, we consider the state of pure nature, we observe that the perfectibility attributed to the man of the state of pure nature is nil in the state of pure nature and without effect there. What I have just said about perfectibility might also be said about freedom, which is the second peculiarly human faculty.

To this point, Rousseau has offered us a certain image of natural man's freedom, something like the identity of subject and substance, of man and nature, an image that mobilized only the concrete givens required by the system. Now, however, we see another determination of freedom suddenly surge up in the text: intellectual freedom, the power to will and to choose, and intellectual awareness of willing and choosing. Here too, we have to do with the same surprise: that which is affirmed about intellectual human freedom is, in the state of pure nature, of no effect and non-existent.[50]

---

50 Cf. 'Nature alone does everything in the activities of a beast while man contributes to his own, in his capacity as a free agent. The beast chooses or rejects by instinct, man by free action.' Ibid., p. 32.

Perfectibility, freedom: Rousseau thus attributes to man original qualities that have the disconcerting feature of being original and non-existent in the state of origin. The same holds for pity. The case of pity is very interesting, inasmuch as it is, according to Rousseau, the sole natural virtue – let us take this to mean the sole natural social faculty prior to reflection and reason – yet a negative social virtue, inasmuch as pity is a feeling that brings a relationship between man and another sentient creature, man or animal, into play; but this relationship is not a positive social relationship. The effect of pity is not to bring men together, but to prevent men from harming other men or animals. That is why Rousseau discusses it in connection with Hobbes, immediately after examining the hypothesis that there exists a sociability based on the desire to do harm.[51] He opposes to it the feeling of the desire not to do harm known as pity. In question here, however, is a simple abstention that is not enough to constitute the beginnings of a society, since it does not bring men together. We may say about pity that it is the concept of relation in non-relation.

Be that as it may, it seems that pity, unlike perfectibility and freedom, is well and truly active in the state of pure nature, that is, the origin, since Rousseau says that it can temper the desire for self-preservation in natural man. However, to this affirmation, which would, moreover, seem to be of no great consequence, since men practically never encounter each other, we may oppose a logic that is internal to the theory of pity. This logic is developed at length in *Emile*. It may be summed up as follows: pity presupposes a complex process in which there intervene, first, a personal experience of suffering, hence a memory of suffering, hence a certain memory of personal suffering and, second, an imaginary identification of the ego that is suffering or has suffered with the ego of others who are suffering at present.[52]

---

51   Ibid., pp. 44–6.

52   'So pity is born, the first relative sentiment which touches the human heart according to the order of nature. To be sensitive and pitiful the child must

This process, however, in order to be possible, brings into play a system of memory, anticipation, projection, and imagination – above all, imagination and abstraction – of which natural man is altogether incapable.

We can, consequently, only conclude that, although Rousseau attributes pity to the state of origin, pity is nil and without effect in the state of the origin, in the state of origin of pure nature, because the conditions of its realization do not obtain.

Here, then, are the elements that constitute the origin. We have, first, the animal nature of man with his faculties and needs, as well as his passion, self-love. This animality is active in the state of nature, in the origin. However, since man is neither sociable nor reasonable, since, by his nature, he does not speak, his animality contains no internal principle of development. Everything has to come to him from the outside.

Next, we have the pity that figures in the origin. It is the relation of non-relation; it is the community of abstention in suffering. Hence it is inactive or even non-existent in the state of nature.

Next, we have freedom, as intellectual power or intellectual awareness. It is inactive and non-existent in the state of nature.

We have perfectibility, the general principle of the possibility, of the virtuality, of the development of all the human faculties. It is by definition inactive in the state of nature.

Of these four elements, one, the first, animality, is immanent in the state of nature and active in the state of nature. It therefore figures in the origin and exists there. The other elements display the paradoxical characteristic of being attributed to the origin without existing in the origin, without functioning there, without producing any effect there, without changing anything at all there. These are, therefore, attributes of the origin that are present by their attribution and absent by their existence.

---

know that he has fellow creatures who suffer as he has suffered.' Rousseau, *Emile*, p. 168.

What do they do in the origin? They are, in the origin, in abeyance [*en attente*], in reserve for later, in order to intervene in the
process of socialization and denaturation and, above all, in order
to intervene in the act of the denaturation of denaturation. We
may say that, by conferring this status of virtuality in reserve on
them, Rousseau has found the way both to respect the separation
of the origin and to get around it. In short, Rousseau has found a
way to think a separate origin which is, after all, an origin, in a very
special mode.

I mean by this that we could level at Rousseau the criticism that
he levels at Hobbes, that of projecting the result onto the origin:
for instance, of projecting freedom and pity, which can be conceived of as social faculties, onto the origin. Rousseau, however,
could reply that neither freedom nor pity plays any role in the
origin and, consequently, does not determine what happens in
the origin or what will emerge from the origin. Freedom and pity
are inscribed in the origin, but they serve no purpose there. They
are inscribed there for later, so that modifications of them may be
inscribed, in their turn, in the process of socialization and denaturation; but, above all, they are inscribed there for their reprise,
their reprise in the denaturation of denaturation, new foundations
in the social contract.

For it is in the social contract that the origin acquires its meaning. It is in the social contract that freedom intervenes, after the
long history of its loss, as an intellectual act in order to invest the
universal dependency of men – the universal dependency of men
resulting from the whole process of socialization – with the meaning of a community based on right [*communauté de droit*]. It is in
the social contract that pity, which has become natural law and
morality thanks to the development of reflection, will intervene to
assign the act that founds the community the objective of equality
and freedom for everyone. It is in the contract – hence at the end
of the risky process constituted by the process of socialization –
that freedom and pity intervene as origin.

At this point, certain things must be made more precise. The form now taken by this intervention of the origin is that of the *reprise*, that is, the form of a new beginning of a beginning; but, nota bene, of a beginning that has never taken place. We can utter this sentence because what is reprised in the contract is freedom and pity as origin, whereas, in the origin, freedom and pity are non-existent. We can utter it, as well, when we recall the enigmatic sentence of Rousseau's in which, referring to the state of pure nature, he writes that it perhaps never existed.[53]

This is perhaps the meaning of the origin in Rousseau from the moment it is subjected to the radical critique of the origin as circle. To be the true origin, distinct from the false origin, it must be separate; this is its first meaning, separation. The figuration of the pure state of nature, as we have seen, is the realization of this separation. To be an origin, however, albeit separate, to be a true origin, the origin must be virtual; to be at once separate and an origin, the synthesis is virtuality. The origin must be virtual, in abeyance, in reserve; it must therefore be non-existent in the positioning of it as origin.

The figuration of the pure state of nature realizes the contradiction just mentioned, that of positing something non-existent as a virtuality for later. This is the second meaning of the origin, that is, a virtuality for later; the first is separation. But, if so, the existing, active origin can only be the real reprise of the origin, the reprise and repetition of the origin, but the reprise of a meaning that has never taken place. The repetition of an event that has never taken place, the new beginning of a beginning that has never taken place, since all that was non-existent in the origin. This is the third meaning of the origin: reprise.

If we go on to ask what this origin as separate, virtual, and reprised might well be, we find another concept to designate it in Rousseau: the concept of *loss*. If the origin has never taken place, it is because it is lost. If it is reprised, if it is the repetition of

53   Rousseau, *Discourse on the Origin of Inequality*, p. 15.

something definite that has never taken place, it is because it is lost. If it repeats that which has not taken place, it is because it repeats what is lost. It is perhaps here, ultimately, that Rousseau is most profoundly self-consistent: in the idea that the loss I just spoke of is consubstantial with the origin.

We can read, black on white, the idea that the loss I just spoke of is consubstantial with the origin in the two contracts of which Rousseau elaborates the theory – this strange redoubling of the contracts: there are two contracts in Rousseau just as there are two origins – the contract that brings the second Discourse to a close and the one that is the subject of the treatise called *The Social Contract*. For what is the contract? It is the reprise of the origin. What becomes of the contract in the second Discourse? We see the ruse of the rich lead to the establishment of laws, and then, after experience demonstrates their disadvantages, to the designation of magistrates, that is, political authorities. And what is the result of this whole process? It is the establishment of despotism, the end of law, a return to the state of war, and so on ad infinitum. This begins over and over again, ad infinitum.

Thus we see how the reprise of the origin is lost, to be reprised again and lost again, without end. Thus we see the circle of the identity of the origin and its loss reconstituted before our very eyes, not at the origin, but in the reprise of the origin, which is, precisely, the whole origin; this in the second Discourse. In *The Social Contract*, we see, behind the dialectic of the universal alienation, in the contract, of the general will and law, another dialectic that is the exact obverse [*envers*] of the first: the dialectic of the death that stalks every body politic and precipitates it into despotism – hence the same loss. The reasoning is different, but the theme is the same.

Here, perhaps, is the point that most overtly opposes Rousseau to the natural law philosophers with respect to the conception of the origin and, by way of the origin, the conception of their theoretical objects and, by way of their theoretical objects, the conception of their relationship to politics.

By 'relationship to politics', I do not just mean declared positions or the political significance of theoretical systems. We know
that Rousseau opposed absolute monarchy and advocated an egalitarian democracy of free and equal small craftsmen living in what
he calls 'independent commerce'. By 'relationship to politics', I
mean that, but I also mean something more, something that distinguishes Rousseau from his predecessors and all his contemporaries
when we take their different positions into account: a certain relationship to his own political positions, a certain way of thinking
and positing his own political theses.

It is by way of this idea that I would like to return, due allow-
ance made, to the words I hazarded about Machiavelli vis-à-vis the
natural law philosophers who, faced with an absolute monarchy
already in power, thought in the accomplished fact, whereas
Machiavelli *thought the fact to be accomplished*.[54] For, due allow-
ance made, Rousseau too, with completely different objectives,
does not think in the accomplished fact; rather, in criticizing the
accomplished fact, he thinks, in a certain way, the fact to be accomplished. To be sure, he, by no means, thinks as a realistic politician,
as Machiavelli does. That is, he does not think this fact to be
accomplished as a practical act to be accomplished, with certain
essential political premises. Rather, he thinks it as a moralist and a
philosopher who tries to adjust theoretical notions in an attempt
to take the measure of a possible essence.

Now here is what I think is important: every possibility always
seems to Rousseau to be suspended over an abyss. Every contract
always seems to Rousseau to be sapped by its own death. Every
reprise [*reprise*] always seems to Rousseau to be condemned to
its own loss. If the origin only exists as lost, although nothing is
ever lost, it is because we must take history as it has made itself
and men as they have made themselves, and then go to work to
re-appropriate it [*reprendre*], to re-appropriate history, in order

---

54 Althusser is referring to a course he gave in January 1972.

to put it on different foundations, yet with no precedent, without benefit of any guarantee whatsoever that might provide protection against death and loss.

This position obviously presupposes a certain view of history and politics and, however paradoxical this may be for someone who never talked about it, a certain view of political action. If we were to go into an analysis of this point, we would discover that what characterizes Rousseau's utopianism, his conception of the fact to be accomplished, is an extraordinarily acute awareness of its necessity and its impossibility, that is, of its precariousness.

That a utopian should criticize accomplished fact, that he should criticize the existing world, is common coin. That a utopian should erect, on his criticism of the accomplished fact, his criticism of the existing world, a utopian theory of the fact to be accomplished, of the world to be constructed – that too is common coin, it is business as usual. But, precisely, the modality that distinguishes Rousseau's thought from that of other utopians is the critical self-consciousness in his utopia itself. It is the criticism brought to bear on the thought of utopia itself at the very moment in which the thought of utopia is thought. It is the origin thought as loss. Thus, among all the reasons that have made Rousseau effective in history, I believe that we must, for theoretical and political reasons, make a rather exceptional place for what is rather exceptional: his critical utopianism – Rousseau's acute awareness of, simultaneously, the necessity, but also the precariousness, of his audacity.

Index

accident, 5, 13, 15, 19, 20, 26, 48, 77, 78, 84, 91, 104
agriculture, 5, 10, 17, 20, 77, 93
Aristotle, 13, 119

Burlamaqui, Jean-Jacques, 36

circle, 12, 14–19, 25–7, 39, 41, 43, 46, 48–51, 53, 54, 56, 59, 64, 66, 70, 77, 79, 80, 86, 89, 91, 98, 105, 106, 108, 121, 133, 137, 138
  of alienation, 46, 49, 50, 51, 66
  of denaturation, 7–9, 17, 26, 46, 50, 59
  of pure nature, 26
  of reason, 51, 59
  of the true origin, 10

Condillac, Étienne Bonnot de, 35
Cournot, Antoine Augustin, 26

Democritus, 24
denaturation, 7–9, 16, 17, 26, 46, 49–56, 59, 66, 68, 69, 76, 104, 136
denaturation of the denaturation, 12, 20, 82, 95–7, 106
Diderot, Denis, 13, 44, 119
  Encyclopaedia, 119
Diogenes, 47

Eden, 4
Engels, Friedrich, 12, 19–22, 96, 100
  Anti-Dühring, 12, 19, 96

Enlightenment, 2, 3, 8, 44, 59
Epicurus, 24

Fondation Gabriel Péri, vii
forest, 4, 11, 13–15, 18, 19, 26,
    76, 85, 86, 93, 107, 116,
    117, 127, 129–31

Glaucus, 47, 48, 55
Goldschmidt, Victor 6
Grotius, Hugo, 36, 41, 44

heart, 7–9, 16, 25–7, 56–61,
    63–71, 81, 86, 87, 99, 134
Hegel, Georg Wilhelm
    Friedrich, 35, 63, 71,
    106–8, 113, 116
    bei sich, 108
    Gestaltung, 84, 106, 107
    Handgreiflichkeit, 113
    Philosophy of Subjective Spirit,
        116
    Schwärmerei, 63
Heidegger, Martin, 24

inequality, 2–7, 13, 14, 18,
    35–7, 39, 47, 65, 71, 73,
    74, 83, 96, 98, 104, 108,
    111, 112, 119–22, 127, 137

Kant, Immanuel, 35

Leclerc, Georges-Louis, count
    of Buffon, 5

Lenin, Vladimir, 21–3
Locke, John, 2, 9, 32, 35, 36, 69,
    73, 75, 82, 94, 127
Lycurgus, 81

Mao Zedung, 22
Martin-Haag, Éliane, 8,
    16
Marx, Karl, 100
    Capital, 12, 96, 99, 100
Marxism, 1, 2, 12, 22, 24,
    25
Marxism–Leninism, 21
materialism, 2, 6, 16, 21–8
Matheron, Alexandre, 29
Matheron, François, vii, 6
Mercier de la Rivière,
    Pierre-Paul, 119
metallurgy, 5, 8, 10, 17, 77, 79,
    93, 104

nature, 1–17, 20, 21, 26, 30, 33,
    34, 36–49, 51, 54–61,
    63–72, 74–90, 92–8, 100,
    104–28, 130, 131, 133–5,
    137
néant, 9, 12, 18, 19, 26, 84, 86,
    106, 118 *see also* nothing-
    ness, void
necessity, 9, 10, 18, 24, 25, 27,
    53, 71, 74, 90, 99, 101,
    111, 121, 140
negation of the negation, 12, 14,
    20, 22, 96, 97, 106

nothingness, 14, 15, 18, 19, 23–6, 28, 33, 48, 118, 130
  see also néant, void

origin, 2–14, 18, 24–6, 33–9, 43–8, 50–7, 59–61, 63–6, 69–74, 76, 80, 82–4, 86–98, 100, 103–8, 111, 112, 117, 120–3, 125, 127, 130, 132–40

Plato, 11, 71, 81, 108, 111
Procreation, 127
Prometheus, 108
Protagoras, 108
Pufendorf, Samuel, 13, 36, 119, 120

reprise, 20, 22, 28, 136–9
Robert Derathé, 3, 38, 120
Rousseau, Jean-Jacques (works)
  Discourse on the Origin and Foundations of Inequality among Men, 2–4, 13–4, 73
  second Discourse, 3, 24, 28, 35–6, 39–40, 63–5, 69, 73, 76, 85, 87, 103, 108, 109, 127, 129, 132, 138
  Emile, 7, 10, 16, 27, 81, 127, 134
  'Essay on the Origin of Languages', 121
  The New Heloise, 16

The Social Contract, 44, 73, 81
Rousseauesque, 3, 7, 10, 11, 13, 23, 35, 132
Rousseauism, 6

savage man, 4, 11, 15, 42, 43
savages, 5, 107, 112, 123
social contract, 2, 12, 20, 34, 74, 76–8, 80–2, 95, 101, 118, 119, 136–9
Spinoza, Baruch, 29
Starobinski, Jean, 3
state
  civil, 37, 39, 42–4, 47, 72, 74, 75, 77, 78, 80, 81, 95
  of nature, 2, 5, 7–11, 16, 17, 26, 33, 34, 36–46, 49, 54, 55, 59–61, 63–9, 72, 74–83, 85, 86, 88, 90, 92–4, 104–7, 112–15, 118, 123, 125, 126, 128, 130, 135, 137
  of pure nature, 3, 8, 9, 12–14, 55, 56, 61, 64–70, 76, 78–90, 92, 94, 95, 104–8, 110, 111, 115–18, 121–4, 130, 131, 133, 134, 137
  of savagery, 66, 67
  of war, 2, 5, 37, 47, 56, 75, 77–82, 90, 91, 93, 94, 100, 104, 125, 138

trees, 13, 15, 16, 107, 108, 114,
117, 129, 131 *see also*
forest

void, 9–12, 14, 15, 17–20,
24–6, 48, 71, 72, 86, 101,

110, 131 *see also* nothingness, void
Voltaire, 4

youth of the world, 4, 5, 10, 12,
14, 17, 20, 76, 77, 80, 93